From the Str

To

With love and thanks

for friendship and help

Flo xxx

C000121326

Also by Florence Jones

Memoirs of a Liverpool Stripper
Published by Pharaoh Press
ISBN 0 9525543 13

From the Stripper with love

FLORENCE JONES

PHARAOH PRESS

From the Stripper with love
ISBN 1901442 071

First Published in 1999 by Pharaoh Press

Conditions of Sale:

Published by Pharaoh Press
Printed by
Stephenson Print, Prescot, Merseyside

Dedication

To my family, Marion, Eric and Erica,
for all their love and support.

· Chapter One ·

"You'll be wantin' a cuppa tea," was the greeting we received in answer to our knock at the door of the house in Corwen, North Wales. "Sit yourselves down. The kettle's on." And the lady bustled away into the kitchen.

"Seems all right," I whispered to my new husband.

She came back with tea and biscuits.

"I'm Mrs Peake," she said, "And this is my husband." Mr Peake was smaller than she was herself. "You're on honeymoon, I can tell."

Blushing, we admitted that we were. In those days, it was something to hide, as though it was immoral.

Leslie and I had been married in a Baptist Church on Sunday 26th September 1937. It had to be on a Sunday because we couldn't afford to lose the pay for two Saturdays. Nobody had paid holidays in those days.

It was a nice wedding. My ex-boss was there and some of the boys from my Sunday School class.

Edie's future Mother-in-Law presided over the refreshments at home. And a good time was had by all. At least, I hope so.

Now we were in Corwen with Mrs Peake, a large lady, very Irish, and her husband who was small and very Welsh. They had two grown-up daughters.

They were a delightful family, taking photos of us with the daughters with the inevitable No 2 Brownie which went everywhere with us. Mrs Peake seemed to anticipate things we needed.

"I'll take you to your room." And she left us to unpack.

Downstairs she said, "I'll explain about the lavatory. You have to give it two sharp tugs on the chain," she told us demonstrating, "otherwise it will give you a shower."

We were just beginning to cope with it when we had to leave, by which time we'd had a few showers and provided the family with laughter. They wished us all the best for the future.

Edie and Tommy were waiting in the house when we arrived home.

"We've decided to get married on Boxing Day," they told us.

"Where are you going to live?"

"At home with Dad."

"Rather you than me."

"There's some post here for you."

It was the rates bill.

"They don't waste any time sending them out." We'd only had the house three weeks.

After they'd gone we were sitting talking when there was a knock at the door.

"We're from next door. We saw you coming in and thought we'd introduce ourselves, Sal and Jim."

We were soon chatting away as though we were old friends which indeed we soon became.

"There's only a few houses taken," Sal said, "it's very quiet."

The gardens were in a terrible state, so at weekends

the men worked on them. Some old houses on the path going into Huyton had been demolished and the trees chopped down.

"I'd like to make an arch for roses," Les told Jim. "We could see if there's anything along the path that we could build it with."

So off they went and came back with bikes laden with branches and started on the arches.

"Amy and Dave have asked us to go for supper tomoorow night."

We'd been there a while when she said, "Would you like some potato cakes?"

"Oh, yes, please," we said, the lads thinking of their mother's delicious ones.

"I'll come with you."

In the kitchen Amy said, "D'you know how to make them?"

"No, don't you?"

She didn't either.

We concocted something between us. They looked all right when they came out of the oven, but they tasted awful. We admitted they were a disaster, but Leslie and Dave never let us forget it. "Made any potato cakes recently?" they'd greet us.

The road started to fill up, mostly with young married couples. Some of them had a mother or a mother-in-law living with them.

It was necessary to go to the shops every day. We had no fridge, of course, but the pantry had a cold slab which was actually the top of the outside coal bunker. We had to use old and tested means of keeping the food fresh. And everything was bought fresh on the day it was to be cooked. Hoping for regular orders, tradesmen brought free samples of bread and milk and a newspaper.

I used to visit Edie once a week because it was too far for her to come to me. We were two tram rides away and then a fifteen minute walk.

Two weeks before Christmas she talked me into making mince pies for her.

"I'll have to do them here," I told her. "You get the ingredients."

As usual, I was running round after her. Yes, even now I was married.

The next time I visited her the ingredients were waiting for me, 3lbs of flour, 1lb of lard. I used all of it, it was an awful lot of dough. After cutting out the pies and using the trimmings there was still plenty of pastry left. It was getting late, and I wanted to be at the tram stop before 4pm when the scramble started. It was a matter of the survival of the fittest then, who could push their way to the front to get on the tram. Many arguments arose from this. One night, one man pushed another who fell on his head and died. The inquest revealed the man had a very thin skull. We were very upset over this, as we knew him.

To go back to the pastry, I rolled the trimmings left after cutting out the pies into a ball and ran down the passage to the backdoor and opened it. Edie's big Alsatian was waiting outside. I threw the ball of pastry and it went down with one gulp. A couple of times more, and it was all gone.

"You can tidy up," I told Edie.

"I've just made a cuppa tea."

"No time!" I was on my way.

A few weeks later Edie told me the dog was dead.

· Chapter Two ·

Although we had been expecting it for months, we seemed to have been lulled into a sense of security, believing it might not happen.

It was a terrible shock to hear the announcement on the wireless:

'Adolph Hitler's troops have invaded Holland and we are now at war with Germany.'

Sal and Jim rushed in from next door.

'Did you hear the news? Isn't it awful.'

It was Sunday morning, so for some people instead of going to church they had to obey the wireless instructions:

'All army personel and voluntary workers report to the nearest depot. Without delay.'

Jim said, 'That's me, Sal.'

'Don't go, Jim,' she said, nearly in tears.

'I have to go. It's the law.'

So she made him wait while she made sandwiches for him to take. He was back in ten minutes and wasn't called again for weeks.

Then another announcement came over the air:

'Keep your wireless set on for further instructions.'

Soon communal Air-raid shelters were going up all over the streets in the town, while in the suburbs each household had its own. Ours was an Anderson put up in the garden. Some people had Morrisons in the front room which they had to crawl under during a raid and sit on the floor. At least we could sit upright in ours.

The next thing to be introduced was the Identity Card.

Elsie, a friend I'd known at work had come to live opposite, called one morning. "We have to get our cards from the Church Hall in Huyton. Comin'?"

So we pushed the prams into Huyton to find a place in the queue. It was like a football match, with people shouting, babies screaming, children running round, prams clutttering the place. We were glad to get home two hours later.

Now we'd been identified we could have ration books.

"Collect them in a few days," they'd told us.

They were buff-coloured for adults, green for children.

"Listen to the wireless," we were told. "You'll find out when to use the ration books. And how."

People who had money were stocking up things like tea, sugar and meat. The shops soon ran out. After all, it had only been twenty-one years since the last war, and they remembered.

We had all been getting to know our neighbours. Now that some of the men were in the Services, and those left behind working all the hours there were in the war effort, the women had to get on with the jobs the men used to do. Most of us had one or two babies so stayed at home to look after them.

The housing estate built for the Pioneer Corps was now occupied. Les went to the ships helping to turn cruisers into troopships. We heard of planes being shot down and ships torpedoed, but on the home front it was being called a phoney war, while Hitler's troops were marching into all the countries around him aided by the Italians. 'The Berlin-Rome Axis' they called it.

Our rations were very sparse. One egg each a week. Two ounces of butter, four of margarine, four of cheese. Four ounces of sugar to begin with. Later everything was rationed except offal and sausages. If word went round that the butcher had got any in, a queue soon formed outside the shop. Those living near the shops were luckiest.

That was one good thing about it, instead of the usual scramble and shouting in the shops and on public transport in the City, people formed orderly queues. Indeed, queueing became a way of life. If you saw a queue, you joined it. There was a story of a lady at the back of a long queue who asked, "What are we queueing for?"

"Tales of Hoffman."

"Oh, how d'ye cook 'em?"

This sort of thing relieved the monotony a bit, as well as the notices around, such as:

Be like Dad – keep mum.

and

Careless talk costs lives.

A wag made up one of his own. It was a drawing of a man's head looking over a wall with the notice, "Chad was here." It was all over the place.

The Pioneer Corps had moved out of the estate to go to France. In their place were interned Italians and Austrians.

It was in 1940 that the first bomb was dropped on the other side of the Mersey.

One night a bomber had passed over the houses in our area. The double buzz of the engine proved it to be German. We all took to the shelters but it passed over without incident.

From then on, the war really started.

Children had been evacuated from the town to safer places. Park railings and some gardens had been taken down to make arms. Shops closed early. And the blackout was complete. We thought we knew our way home, but getting off the tram in the dark one night and walking the ten minutes we reached the house, I found I'd lost my wool.

"Look, I've dropped my ball of wool." Les went back to look for it. "It was right by the tram stop and wound round all sorts of things like trees and the buckets of sand at the end of the roads." They were to help put fires out, whem the bombing started, as we knew it would.

Those men who were still at home and single women were recruited for fire-watching after work.

The pattern was set for the next five years. Other cities were already being bombed. It would be Liverpool's turn next.

· Chapter Three ·

The May blitz had started with the sight of the flames raging up to the sky from the docks. From then on it was queueing in the day and the shelter at night. Sometimes it was after we'd gone to bed that the siren sounded. Then we'd have to grab blankets and the baby, shrug into dressing gowns and go down to the shelter.

As time went on, the siren went off earlier and earlier. Then it was a hurried dinner so that we'd be ready. Listening to the bangs, Marion would clap her hands over her ears and shout "Duck! Duck!" When at last the All Clear went, we'd crawl out of the shelter like snails from their shells, and flop into bed for what was left of the night.

The wardens used to come round calling, "Everyone all right?"

Most of them were very good, but as usual, some took their duties as though we were all in school, shouting "Put that light out!" although it was so small they could only see it by peering through the letter box. One man was so annoyed, he shouted back at the warden, "If you're not careful someone will put your light out."

All our neighbours were very friendly and helped one another. A knock at the door and a shout, "There's bananas in Waterworths!" Or sausages at the butcher's. Or liver. Then you'd stop everything and dash down to the shops, and if you were lucky maybe get a banana for the child as some always had to be set aside for children.

One morning after a night's bombing, my friend Hilda came round. "Can you leave the baby with Elsie and come with me to town?"

"What's the hurry?"

"They've got prams in Lewis's."

Hilda was pregnant and had been trying to buy a pram for a time. Even second-hand ones were scarce.

Alighting from the tram in town, utterly bewildered, we looked at one another and said together, "Where are we?" There was devastation all around us. We stood wondering which way to go, lost. Threading our way through the rubble of glass, wood, bricks, and the ruined contents of shops we finally reached the pram place.

"You're lucky!" Hilda was told. "We only had two prams in, and one's gone already."

With no-one knowing what the next night might bring, all the shops sold out very quickly. Our trip down the town to fetch Hilda's pram made us realise just how lucky we were to be living on the outskirts. When people started leaving Liverpool for safer places nobody could blame them.

There was a popular song about soldiers coming home on leave. It went,

Bless 'em all, bless 'em all,
The long and the short and the tall.
Bless all the sergeants and W.O.Is.
Bless all the corporals and their blinkin' sons.
For they're saying Goodbye to them all

As back to their billets they crawl.
They'll get no promotion
This side of the ocean,
So cheer up my lads,
Bless 'em all.

Now a parody was doing the rounds.

Bless 'em all, bless 'em all,
The long and the short and the tall.
Bound for West Kirby and Hoylake and Meols,
Llandudno Junction and Llanidrod Wells.
For we're saying Goodbye to them all
As back to their funk-holes they crawl.
You'll get bombs up your jersey
This side of the Mersey.
So cheer up my lads,
Bless 'em all.

Which wasn't very fair because whoever had written it would probably have done the same if they'd been able to.

When the winter started in earnest, going anywhere was a risk. With the days so short, there was always the problem of getting home before dark. Before the sirens went. One good thing about it was there was no scramble in shops or on the buses. Just orderly queues. This was a new development, and had never been known before.

The two years we'd been married made me realise that courting and marriage were very different things. Now we had to get to know one another properly.

Leslie's mother had always waited on him hand-and-foot. I'd known he had a stubborn streak.

There was the business with the parrot, for instance. The parrot had been brought home by an uncle who'd been at sea. The cage hung above Leslie's chair at the table. He was always complaining about it. "It sneezes. It sneezes all over me." But no matter how much of an irritation the parrot was, Leslie wouldn't move his chair. "I was here first," he'd say. "I'm not moving."

"Well we're not moving the cage," his father used to say. "It's the only place for it."

And there it stayed, with Leslie sitting underneath it, grumbling. Until a friend who owned an inn in the country took it off their hands. So I suppose he could say he'd won in the end.

We'd been talking about this. "You're still as stubborn," I told him.

Before he could answer, the siren went, and we were back in the shelter. It was at the bottom of the garden. It was flooded, we found. The wooden floor Leslie had made to keep us dry was afloat. We spent a very uncomfortable night.

"What's happened?"

"The heavy rain today has made the water from all around flood into the hole because the soil is mostly clay."

"Great! What do we do now?"

"We'll have to move the shelter towards the house."

The next night was even worse, we were practically paddling. Eventually the shelter was moved and no water seeped in afterwards. At least, if it did we were well above it.

We often had arguments. One night I was so annoyed over something, I bundled the baby into a coat. "I'm going back home," I told him.

"Don't be daft."

Just as I opened the front door, my friend Ella was coming up the path. "Are you going out?"

"No, I'm just coming in."

Leslie sat grinning all night. Later, after he'd seen Ella to the tram stop in the black-out, it was all forgotten and we went on as before.

· Chapter Four ·

Rationing was very hard on everyone, but for people like my mother-in-law who was a wonderful cook and always produced sumptuous meals, it was especially hard. Although she'd had a good supply in at the start, it didn't last very long.

She decided to do something about it.

She ran a card school. She and four friends and the next-door neighbour used to play Newmarket (*see footnote*). We joined in sometimes and found it hilarious.

They played for ha'pennies, and we all knew who would have the queen.

"Who's got the jack?"

"It's in the dummy hand."

"Play the ten then."

If that didn't come out she had the queen too, and we all knew who had it. Sometimes there'd be as much as sixpence on the queen.

They'd never be able to play Poker!

Anyway, before the war Leslie's mother had spent holidays in a cottage in Wales. Now with her card school cronies, she hired a car for the day and went to visit Mrs

Now in June 1998 as I check through this before it goes to the publisher, I thought I'd look at the book of card games we have for our crosswords and find out how Newmarket was played. Their version was very similar to ours – like us they used two packs of cards, one to be dealt to the players, the other one

Owen in her cottage in Wales, coming back with eggs, ham and sometimes bread.

The eggs were put into water with isinglass, a kind of gelatine, to preserve them. And although she was terrified of being found out breaking the law, she still kept on doing it.

"We'll be asked to show what we're carrying."

But they never were.

Then came the real scarey journey. They came back from Mrs Owen's with half a pig. It was illegal to kill an animal without permission.

Everybody that came to the door was vetted, just in case he was an inspector. We had some lovely meals with our share of it. Mother-in-law was relieved and sighed with joy when it was all safely disposed of. Still, it was great while it lasted, that Welsh pig.

Although our house was on a new estate, I met many friends from school and work there, and even some church people.

Margery, my friend from school, was a very clever dressmaker. Our clothes coupons had to be spent on the children, so when Margery said, "I love this coat, but I'm getting too fat for it."

I said, "It's a lovely coat. I'll buy it."

It was a perfect fit. When Margery was slim again she bought the coat back. And later, I had it again, still good.

They don't make them like that any more.

My husband had a habit of dashing to the back door whenever there was a sound of a plane. Then he'd come back and say, "It's all right – it's one of ours."

"You'll be saying that once too often," I told him. And sure enough, he came rushing in at about five o'clock one afternoon.

"Quick! Into the shelter. There's gunfire."

A plane had come very low and was shooting the people in the street.

As usual, in the midst of gloom something happens to lighten it. A lorry full of sugar sacks going to the town was spilling sugar from a hole in a sack. People ran out onto the road with buckets, bags, tin pans. Men in smart suits took off their bowlers and their trilby hats to hold under the teeming sugar whenever the lorry stopped in the traffic. Strangely enough, nobody was hurt, although it came very close. One smartly dressed business man unrolled his umbrella (a sight that hasn't been seen for years) and held it under the stream of sugar just as the traffic was beginning to move. I couldn't help imagining how he'd be able to transfer his ill-gotten gains into containers after walking through the streets with an umbrella full of sugar. But that was *his* problem.

As the war went on, everything seemed to be rationed. We were introduced to shark fish, whale meat (and that was fishy too). We got used to cooking with dried milk, dried eggs. Friends exchanged bread coupons, say, for cheese. In fact we swapped everything that we could possibly manage without. We were told to Dig for Victory, but in 1941 all this was very far away.

Nights of the Blitz, a lot of big stores and Government buildings were reduced to rubble so that it was impossible to replace anything.

Dyeing and bleaching became an art. I still have a

tablecloth made from a flour sack with lace round the edge. It is pristine white, but when you hold it up to the light, you can see the faint outline of the miller's name printed on it.

Making up a dye to brighten curtains or cushion covers, anything that would take it, was not as straight forward as it is today. Unfortunately all the items that went into the dye did not turn out the same shade.

I once dyed a pair of shoes to go to a funeral. I used a strong smelling radium dye. At the funeral I was seated next to a wide heating pipe. Soon people around me were sniffing. I tried to look as though I knew nothing about it. What a relief it was to move out into the fresh air for the burial.

"Did you know it was me?" I asked a friend afterwards.

May had moved into a Napiers bungalow built for workers in the arms factory. Before I was married myself, I'd sometimes minded her two children for her. Now she had six.

"Still into politics?" I asked her.

"Yes, more so than before. Stan's a councillor."

"Let's hope things are better when this is over."

"Well, it surely couldn't be worse."

"I'm just going to have a bath in my six inches of water."

"Very generous, aren't they."

With that we parted.

· Chapter Five ·

I didn't expect marriage to be like the romances in Peg's Paper or the Netta Musket stories (these were the Mills & Boons of the time). But what did I get? A baby in the first year. I knew nothing about babies. And having no mother, there was no-one I could ask for help or advice. I just had to get on with it as best I could.

Life should have been easier. After all, we were supposed to have come up in the world. We had a dinning room instead of a kitchen, a sitting room in place of a parlour. Not a lobby, but a hall. And instead of a back yard we had a garden.

The weather was against us too. Ours being the last road on the estate, it was open to the elements. It was so cold that in winter a tap left dripping ever so slightly overnight would have a long icicle hanging from it in the morning. One night the cold was so intense, I had to get up out of bed and walk round to keep the circulation going. Next day we took a bucket of coal upstairs, and after that on very cold nights we'd put the remains of the downstairs fire on a shovel and take it up to the bedroom grate. The embers were always smokey, and carrying them upstairs didn't do much for the decorations, but at least we weren't going to freeze in our bed.

As far as marriage and motherhood went, I felt I'd been thrown in at the deep end, and that was before the war started. What an upheaval. Still, I don't suppose I was the only one who felt like that. We all just had to get on with it.

Edie was pregnant again and she wasn't very pleased. Tommy was away in the Army in some remote part of England. I called to see her one day when it was nearly time for the birth. She was in a state. Her three year old son, Peter, had climbed onto an air-raid shelter in the street, fallen off and fractured his skull.

"He's being transferred to Alder Hey Hospital," she said. "Can you go and visit him, Flo?"

I agreed, as usual. But when I got home I found Marion and her little friend Donald from over the road were playing on our air-raid shelter, jumping off it. Suddenly there was a scream, and Marion had broken her leg. We ended up in hospital on our own account, and it was a different one altogether, miles from Alder Hey.

Next day a message came to me, that Edie's baby had come and she was in yet another hospital, in a different direction altogether from the other two.

Ella called that night, and I recruited her to go and visit Peter. The strict rules of visiting allowed me to see Marion for a brief time and afterwards I was able to go on and visit Edie, though this involved two tram rides in each case. A few buses ran from Prescot to Liverpool on the main road and they sometimes went on to Whistan Hospital. Being unfamiliar with the one going that way, I boarded a bus and asked the conductor, was it going to the hospital?

"You women make me sick," he said. "You'd get on an oil barrel if one came along."

Shocked, I said, "Yes, I would if it was going to the hospital."

As I got off the bus, a lady was saying in a loud voice, "Who rattled his cage?"

It was bad enough having to trail all the way to the hospital, without people like him to deal with.

Eventually everything was sorted out. Edie had a daughter, she called her Barbara.

When Marion came home from hospital, she seemed no worse for her accident. She was soon climbing everywhere again. And pulling the heads off the flowers. And helping me to bring in the coal, carrying it in the skirt of her dress if I didn't watch her. Particularly when she had a white dress on.

Leslie's sister, Olive, came to tell me that she had a day off.

"Should we go to New Brighton?"

So we went on the ferry, and had a happy day looking at the shops. We couldn't go on the beach. It was fenced off with barbed wire in case of an invasion. Marion was disappointed.

"It's not always like this, love."

Sitting in a cafe sharing a pot of tea, Olive was feeling round the outside of her cup.

"If you're looking for the handle, there isn't one."

"Well, that's awful! We know how hard it is to get decent stuff, but that's going too far."

"We'll have to make our dishes last."

It was a nice change to get away, have a smell of the sea air, even if it was only for a few hours.

Olive worked in a printers. It was an old building. She kept her sandwiches on a shelf behind the ledger. Reaching up for them one lunchtime, she thought the packet of sandwiches felt surprisingly light. The sandwiches had disappeared. The paper had been gnawed through. A rat.

"They're from the bombsite," she was told.

Every night we turned the Wireless on for the the news. At this stage of the war it wasn't often good news. Sometimes the traitor, Lord Haw Haw (William Joyce) would come on air telling us all kinds of rubbish. Asking us to persuade the government to give in to Hitler. As if we could do anything, any of us! Even if we'd wanted to.

"Jarmany calling . . ." he'd begin. In the end it was just a laugh. Nobody took him seriously.

Then the official government spokesman would come on, telling us how well everything was going for the allies. We believed it until Dunkirk.

"You won't be able to go to New Brighton for a while," my Father-in-law said. "At least not on the Iris or the Daffodil."

"Why not?"

"Because they've gone to Dunkirk. To help our men get away from France. Every boat is needed to help, no matter how small. To rescue the soldiers from the beaches."

They did come back, The Iris and The Daffodil. And the word *royal* was added to their names. In recognition of their splendid war service.

· Chapter Six ·

When I came home from the hospital with the baby, the dog Angus was waiting for me, but at a sound from the baby his ears shot up and he went and sat by the gate. He did this every day and as people passed they'd say, "Had your nose pushed out, eh" Angus was so jealous that when Marion was walking, he attacked her and had to go. Marion still doesn't like dogs!

Her Dad and I like all animals, especially birds. We were so thrilled to see the different ones that visited the garden that Les made a nest box for the blue tits while I threaded peanuts on strings and watched the birds coming down onto the bird table for them.

In those days, thrushes and blackbirds sang every morning, but now there's very few of them because with the building of motorways the magpies come and take the eggs and the chicks. This year we didn't see any, not like the first year when eight bluetits got away. The sprays to kill the insects don't help either. A robin and a wren do still come in the winter.

Leslie had kept budgies in the shed until seed had stopped coming. He tried to feed them on oatmeal and they died. "I'll start again when this lot's over," he declared. But he didn't. He just bought one in a cage and over the years we've had many talkers.

Although there were no paid holidays we managed to

have a week away. The first one was in Blackpool. It wasn't a success. What with rain and wind, and only a go-chair for the child with no cover on it – it was really only a seat on wheels. We had to use towels to try to keep her dry. She was two and took a dislike to the identity bracelet everybody was advised to wear then in case of accidents. But would she wear it? No! Although we pleaded, coaxed and even threatened her, it was no use. She kept dragging the bracelet off.

The next holiday was even worse. We went to Prestatyn in North Wales. The first night we were there, the bucket and spade I'd managed to get was put under the bed. In the middle of the night the bed collapsed and squashed the bucket flat. Not that it mattered – the beach was all tank traps and barbed wire.

The landlady was a huge woman dressed in black. She sat in the kitchen opposite the front door watching everything that went on. One day we were standing by the front door watching the teeming rain when she came up behind us and said, 'Would you like an umbrella?' We took the hint and went out.

We met a young boy who asked, "Are you staying at number 17?"

"Yes. Why?"

"I thought so. I lodge there. I have to sleep in the shed when she has visitors."

"She's like a big black spider with her three big fluffy Persian cats," I told him.

"You won't get enough to eat. She's very mean. Look, this is what I do." And he showed us his pockets full of apples.

"Why d'ye stay here?"

"I work in the cafe training to be a chef."

We had a sample of her stinginess when a neighbour called and asked for a few apples to make a pie for visitors.

"I'll see if there's any windfalls," she said, though the trees were laden with apples.

When we arrived, she had asked for the ration books right away, of course. But there was never enough to eat. We were like Oliver Twist, always asking for more. There was always an argument.

"You go . . ."

"No, you go."

You can guess who had the job – me.

Another couple came next day. In their case it was the man who did the asking, and he seemed to get more out of the landlady than I did so at tea-time I gave Leslie the jug.

"It's your turn to ask."

He came back with a jug-full.

"She nearly jumped out of her skin when she saw me," he said.

"You can go again."

One day we all happened to go out at the same time. We got back first.

"Eh, this is great," we said when we saw the table set with enough bread, 4 medium-sized tomatoes and a jar of meat-paste. Leslie ate two of the tomatoes. Marion never having seen meat-paste before polished off the jar.

Then the other couple came in and went to ask for their teas.

"It was set out for you all. You went out together, I reckoned you'd eat your tea together."

We'd scoffed the lot.

"You're lucky," I told them. "I don't like tomatoes."

Another day John said, "I looked in the dinning-room and two of the cats were on the table."

"That settles it," his wife said. "We're going home."

"Are they still there?" I asked him.

"Yes, and she is sitting there in the doorway."

"Lend me your newspaper." I went in and having shut the door behind me, belted the cats. When I opened the door again, they went flying out.

"We're not going," I said to Leslie. "We paid as soon as we arrived. Except for the dinners, we won't eat them but she'll still have to make them. Her milk and bread will be all right, I think. We'll find somewhere else more suitable for meals."

Now I love cats, but the idea of those monsters on the table with the food still makes me shudder. We stuck it out until the last minute. The boy came and saw us off.

"You're the only ones to stand up to her," he told us. "Most people leave early."

"I hope you get your room back."

"Did <u>you</u> get your ration cards back?"

"Of course."

So we left the spider and her hen-pecked husband. He hadn't had very much to say. It seems they'd won the Pools and bought a boarding house to escape the bombs.

It was back to the grindstone for us. We certainly would-n't go there again. But at least for that week there'd been no raids to put up with. No rushing for shelters, no bomb scares.

In our district there had been only one bomb, a small one that took the roof off two houses. But a quarter-of-a-mile away one large one fell just as Leslie was on his way home from work.

He came in in a great lather. "I heard the whistle and peddled like mad."

"The child fell out of the pram today," was all I said.

"You don't seem to realise I could have been killed."

A row of houses had been shattered, and the main road was strewn with bricks and tiles, but luckily no-one was hurt.

A good home-coming.

· Chapter Seven ·

After a bout of illness which kept me in bed, we got a woman in to help with the housework. When I saw her washing round the mat in the kitchen (such a small kitchen too!) she had to go. My friend Hilda found me a gem, Ethel, the sister of the woman who was helping her after the birth of her baby.

Ethel knew someone who worked in Hawkins, a textile warehouse supplying materials to the big shops. It was hit by a fire bomb. Some of the bales of cloth were salvaged by cutting the ends off them and selling the rest cheaply. It was mostly cotton. She managed to get some of it for me.

"It's a change from parachute stuff," Ethel said. "And no coupons."

Having help in the house gave me time to read. A branch library had been opened in one of the new shops. The Librarian and I soon became good friends. She saved any new books that came in. On anything and everything.

As I paid all the bills, I scraped and saved to join Foyles Book Club, juggling the money from one bill to another, hoping they wouldn't all come at the same time.

We had few luxuries, but one was biscuits at fivepence ha'penny a pound. I sometimes got a quarter of more expensive ones, but when I did no matter where I hid them Leslie would produce them when we had a cup of tea. Telling his mother about it, she said, "You could never keep anything from him. When he was a child he'd study the crumbs and say, 'You've had cream slices.' "

Leslie was very strict about debt. While other people finished their houses, our rooms were empty. We regretted it later.

When would I have anything better? I felt it was my fault. Things would have been so much easier if we hadn't had to pay the doctor all the time who never sent bills but demanded money right away. This doctor was new to the district, taking the place of one who'd turned out to be an alcoholic. He'd come straight from a hospital in London and was very keen to build up the practice. He wouldn't start work in the morning until the waiting room was full. He'd look in to see how many were waiting, then go away again.

"What's 'e doin'?"

"Feedin' 'is chickens."

"Must be fond of eggs."

"Well, it *is* war time."

"No wonder they call us *patients*! You have to be very patient with him."

When our turn came and we actually got into the surgery, there was a chicken in a box by the fire.

"It's not very well," he told us.

I tried not to complain, because it was hard for my husband too. His mother had always done everything for him. Now he had all this responsibility to contend with.

He hated hospitals. When he was only nine years old, he had contracted scarlet fever and was sent into hospital, enduring six weeks of isolation and never allowed to see anyone except an uncle who had talked his way in and left a bunch of black grapes for the child. A nurse took them away. They were always very keen on bowel movement. Next day he was asked if he'd been to the lavatory. When he said no, the nurse gave him a dose of liquorice and then *one* black grape. He didn't say no again. He never received any of the things his family sent in for him. When at last it was time for him to go home, except for the soles of his feet, all the skin had peeled off him. They scraped it off with some sort of instrument. After such an experience, I could understand why he didn't like hospitals, though when I was in hospital Leslie came in every night to see me after work.

Leslie's mother decided to go on holiday to boost up the black market supplies. She took Marion with her and Lorna the cousin who was a couple of years older. The village they went to was very Welsh. Prisoners of war were billeted there. The two children became very friendly with them.

Out with their grandmother one day, one of the prisoners called out in a lilting Welsh accent, "Hello, you British b******!"

She was horrified, of course, and chased him away, while the Welshmen working in the field were highly amused. They'd taught the prisoners that this was the proper way to greet people.

Besides Germans and Italians, other nationalities were there, and one girl who lived in the village with only her father took full advantage of the amenities and had a baby every year while the war lasted. She could have been called a regular League of Nations all on her own.

I was surprised when my father started to come visiting once a week. He'd always leave before Leslie got home from work. Father had always disapproved of me, more so as I grew up. And he didn't get on with Leslie.

As he left he'd always make the same excuse: "The trams are busy later."

Dolly never came, although she'd have liked the garden. She used to plant flowers in the back yard, taking up some of the sets to expose the soil underneath. She never bothered with any of us. It was like we'd never existed. And they say blood's thicker than water. Ours wasn't.

I'd been a nervous wreck when Marion was born, but constantly worrying about everything as I did, I thought the child would be as bad. So I made a big effort to alter which was just as well because there was a shock to come which tried my nerves and patience to the limit.

· Chapter Eight ·

The first two years after we were married, we went to my family for Christmas Day. I made a lot of mince pies. Edie had all the ingredients ready when I called a few days before and persuaded me to make them. Again I'd obeyed the government's instructions and 'kept mum' with a guilty feeling that it might have been the pastry, though the dog had seemed to enjoy it, swallowing it down in one gulp.

Everything seemed to be going smoothly now, with Edie keeping house for Dad with a friend helping her. No sign of any trouble brewing, any change. The only hint Edie ever gave was when she said, "Dolly's still the favourite with Dad even though she doesn't live here."

About a month after Christmas, Father was still visiting us. One day a van drew up outside the house. Two men moved a bed, a piano, an organ and a few other things into our house.

Dad had come to stay!

It turned out that Dolly and Edie had argued over something and Edie had walked out. She'd gone to her mother-in-law's over the road and arranged to stay there. Dad and Dolly had decided that I had plenty of room for him and his furniture, so without further ado there he was on the doorstep and all his worldly goods with him.

How on earth would I explain Dad's arrival to Leslie when he came in from work? I tried to be diplomatic, but the first thing Leslie said was, "How long is he staying?"

"I don't know."

"You must have known something about it."

"No, I'd not the faintest idea. Dolly's arranged it all without consulting us."

Leslie needed a lot of convincing. "We got married without things we needed because of all the work you did and now you're in a worse position."

It was a very difficult time. Dad smoked an evil pipe. He teased the child. He butted in on conversations so that if we wanted any privacy the only place to go was the bedroom.

Thinking childbirth was a natural event, a woman's lot, Dad wasn't a bit sympathetic about my illness. Hadn't his own mother had seventeen children? Seventeen or eighteen, it made little difference. In his opinion, my duty was to be up in the morning in time to cook my husband's breakfast, instead of having tea taken up to me in bed. Dolly was always up in the morning, he'd tell me. Dolly was so much more capable.

"Does Dolly knit? Does Dolly sew?" I'd sometimes ask him, in self-defence.

"She hasn't the time, what with everything else that she does."

I often had to grit my teeth (my *false* teeth – I'd had to have them all out during pregnancy) and go out into the garden singing to myself a useful song for this sort of situation that we'd learnt at school:

Keep on looking for the bright bright skies,
Keep on hoping that the sun will rise,
Keep on singing when the whole world sighs,
And you'll get there in the morning.

To be honest, I couldn't often see my bright morning coming. Things seemed to be getting steadily worse. One day, after a terrible argument, Leslie said, "We can't go on like this. He's going to wreck our lives."

"Well tell him to go, then."

"He's not my father. You'll have to tell him."

"You don't think I'm enjoying being pig-in-the-middle, do you?"

"Anyway, it's up to you."

So I found the courage to tell him it wasn't working, all of us living together. "You'll have to go back and live with Dolly, Dad."

Which he did. And I never saw either of them again.

The nightmare was over. Now we could start to live again. He'd left the huge organ and the piano behind, but that didn't seem to matter now.

I can't describe the relief I felt to have the house to ourselves again. To be able to talk and even quarrel sometimes anywhere we liked. Perhaps now I could be ill in comfort too.

Among other things, Dad had told Leslie not to buy me chocolates when I was poorly, but butterscotch. The pound of them Leslie bought me I nearly threw at him. Whenever I was taken ill, Dad's diagnosis was the same: "She will be ill, she eats too many chocolates." As it was war time and sweets were rationed, this didn't make much sense.

One day, I'd promised to go over the road to Elsie's. Her boy Donald and Marion were great friends and always played together. Elsie had made us a precious cup of tea, and we sat down to drink it while the children played in the garden.

"It's gone very quiet," I said. "I'll go and see what they're up to."

The back door was open and the children had gone.

We dashed out into the road, but they were nowhere to be seen. We searched in all the places where they might have been and were leaning on the wall exhausted just debating whether or not to go to the Police Station (a shop in Huyton manned by just one constable), when Elsie said, "Look!"

Coming up the road with a child on each arm was a neighbour, a man we didn't like very much. We rushed up to them.

"You should take more care of your children."

"We've been searching everywhere."

"Pity you didn't look in the right place. They were playing on the tramlines at the terminus."

"Thanks for bringing them home."

"I feel like a criminal," I said as we took them indoors.

"So do I," said Elsie. "I'll warm that tea up for us. Can't waste it."

"From now on, we won't have to let them out of our sight."

The next episode happened in our garden. The children were playing out there one morning, when Elsie came for Donald.

"They're in the garden," I told her.

"Just look at them!" she said coming back with them both in tow.

They were covered in soot. From head to foot. What a sight! I'd forgotten that after the sweep had been, he'd left a pile of soot at the bottom of the garden. They'd found it, of course, and had a grand time paddling in it.

I stripped Marion's clothes off, filled the sink with water and plonked her in it. It took a lot of soap and a lot of scrubbing, but she came clean eventually.

I was afraid Elsie would blame me and take umbrage again, but she didn't. Which was just as well as that wasn't the last of their escapades.

Elsie had agreed to mind Marion one day when I had to go into Huyton. I'd scarcely left Marion there, when Elsie was over at our house with both children.

"Look what Marion's done," she said indignantly. "She's cut his curl off!"

Elsie had carefully nurtured Donald's blond hair into a big curl on the top of his head. It was no longer there.

"That's very naughty," I scolded Marion after Elsie had gone. "Where did you get the scissors?"

"Donald climbed on the chair and got them out of the drawer. Anyway, it's not fair. He 'ad two goes at my hair, didn't he."

That finished off my outing.

· Chapter Nine ·

The first Christmas we decided to spend on our own was like a repeat from twenty years earlier, but this one was worse because most luxuries were very difficult to obtain, if you weren't 'in the know', as the saying went. "It's like trying to get corn in Egypt," a Biblical friend told me.

We already had a small tree with a few baubles, so we were making lanterns, paper chains, anything to cheer the place up a bit. Toys were almost impossible to obtain. In the summer I'd managed to buy a small dolls pram. It was just four wheels and a frame with blue canvas and a handle. I had to take it with me as it was as nothing was wrapped then. Unfortunately Marion was with me and as she was never fond of walking she insisted on sitting in it, a tight squeeze. In the ten minute walk from the tram she'd pushed her feet through the bottom and left me exhausted from the effort of stooping down to push it.

So we started making our own toys – dolls and teddy bears – using precious clothing coupons to buy bright coloured wool and scraps that we had for the clothes. While at the docks the men repairing and altering ships for the troops in between sailings used any spare time and oddments of wood (and not necessarily spare) to make toys. They made trains, forts, aeroplanes and jumping jacks (two sticks with elastic threaded between them and in the middle a monkey. When the sticks were squeezed together the monkey did acrobatic tricks). The most popular of the wooden toys were the ducks which were painted yellow and made so that when they were put at the top of a slope they waddled down flapping their wings.

As Christmas approached, the dolls pram was brought out in the evening after Marion was in bed and painted and repaired and it looked fine.

To make things a bit festive we tried to buy crackers but could only get the bangers, so we made our own, all prettied up. The paper was too strong and they resisted all attempts to pull them.

Then there was the cake, short of eggs but with plenty of fruit, a donation from my Mother-in-law, who had received a food parcel from the Orange Order in Canada. Leslie had insisted on making the icing with caster sugar and gelatine. It looked really good if you ignored the spelling which read 'A Meery Christmas.'

When the great moment arrived to cut into it, the icing was rock hard and had to be chiselled off. Still the cake was a luxury to savour when we released it from the icing.

The winters were always very bad and they seemed to last a very long time. If it wasn't raining it was snowing, but the children loved it, making snowmen and slides for the unwary to slip on. But the spring always came in the end with blossom on the trees in the main road, cherry and almond blossom. No matter what was happening in the war, it always lifted my heart to see it. Later on the swifts came back from their winter homes and they could be seen diving and swirling for flies. The nesting box Leslie had made for the bluetits was soon occupied.

Now was the time to shop at leisure and catch up on

the gossip. How certain people were going out with Yanks from Burton Woods in the Wirral while their husbands were away. Most of us never saw a Yank, but we heard all about them.

Now we could get into the garden. We'd grown very fond of gardening. We'd started with the roses given to us by Leslie's brother Arthur who had a garden too. I had pot plants and was fascinated by the different varieties. At home, my Mother had always had aspidistras. She used to wipe over the leaves with milk to keep them glossy. With presents from friends and family, I soon had quite a collection of house plants.

In 1944 Marion started school. She screamed at parting from me. There was no preparation for five-year-olds as there is today to ease them into the new routine. Most of the children cried that first day, but when she came home at lunch-time Marion said, "You needn't come back with me. I'll go meself."

One of the teachers came from Wigan and taught singing. I heard Marion singing "Blow away the mornin' due." Copying the accent, which she can still do. Anything for a laugh!

In 1945 I began to get very breathless, but the doctor said, "You're getting old."

My Mother-in-law had been worried about me, and she was very indignant. "I'll take you to my doctor," she decided.

When she told him the tale he said, "Well, I'm seventy-four and if anyone told *me* that I'd be annoyed, never mind saying it to you at your age!" (I was thirty-four.) "You should change to another doctor."

He arranged for me to go into the Heart Hospital, a private charity owned by a Doctor Harris. The corporation paid for most patients' treatment.

It was a terrible place. The Matron and nurses had noisy parties after lights out. If anyone protested about anything they'd give the usual excuse, "There's a war on."

Visiting was strictly limited. Our vistors were quickly relieved of all gifts of food. We the patients never saw any of it.

"Don't bring any more stuff in for us," we told family and friends. "The staff take it for their nightly orgies."

The place was filthy. Mice ran round at night. Floors were never swept. Every complaint produced the same answer: "We haven't got the staff." Where do we hear that today? Excuses never change.

One day there was a great deal of activity. Beds were smartened and someone said, "Are we going to be done up as well?"

"The Lord Mayor is coming. Dr Harris is hoping he'll make a donation."

The doctor never interfered in the running of the hospital. He was only interested in the patients. The Lord Mayor did come and insisted on being examined himself.

"Your heart's in the right place," Dr Harris told him.

And he was right. The Council did indeed make a contribution to the running of the hospital. But unfortunately a few weeks later the Mayor had a heart attack and died.

When peace was declared, I was still in hospital. It was to be September 1945 before we were all together again and could celebrate properly.

· Chapter Ten ·

It was good to leave the hospital. Marion was staying with her Grandmother, and when we went to collect her Marion said, "We're going to the Isle of Man for a week."

"It'll give you a chance to get back to normal."

I was very grateful, and appreciate my Mother-in-Law's kindness even more now that I'm old myself and realising how much work there is looking after a lively child.

Two days after they'd gone an urgent message came to us: "Send her wellingtons." It rained every day, with a really bad thunderstorm while they were on the boat coming home. They hadn't been worried or scared. The school in Liverpool Gran had sent her to seemed to be very good and as there was one not far away from us, I took Marion there instead of to the Rohy one, explaining as I had before that she was left-handed and must not be made to use the right hand, which is what the schoool had done many years before with her uncle.

In July we had a week at the cottage in Ysbyty Ifan, the village where we'd stayed before. The prisoners-of-war had all gone, and the village seemed to have returned to its quiet ways.

Mrs Owen who prepared the cottage for us said, "I can let you have half-a-dozen eggs off the ration."

Along with other things we'd taken a large packet of porridge oats. The next day we'd eaten most of the stuff we'd taken with us, and went down the hill to the shop.

"The bread's not in yet," we were told.

It still wasn't in at one o'clock. So we ate porridge again.

"It'll be in at five."

But we couldn't wait that long, so we walked the three miles to Pentrefoelas, a small town with a church, a pub and a cafe – wonderful! But still no shop. After walking the three miles back we were ravenous so it was porridge again. The bread finally came in at 7 o'clock.

On the way out one day Mrs Owen brought us a rabbit.

"It'll need a lot of cooking," she warned me.

And it certainly did! It was like leather.

"Did she say Tom Owen had shot it this morning?"

Every morning her husband and some of the other men went out shooting rabbits and sold them at a shilling each in the market.

"I think this one had given itself up."

"Thursday is market day in Llanruist," Mrs Owen told us. "If you want to go, you'll have to be early. The bus only holds fifty."

We left Marion with Mrs Owen and at nine o'clock we were outside Roberts' garage. There was nobody else in sight. At five past the doors opened and the bus rolled out. It was already full to capacity! We were turning away when Mr Roberts said, "There's plenty of room." He brought out a lemonade box and set it down so that we could sit on it back-to-back. The bus was crowded with people nursing boxes of plants, chickens and ducklings, baskets of eggs, jars of jam and pickles. The people talked in Welsh while the chickens chirped and the ducklings squarked.

Large farmers were sitting on either side of me, overhanging their seats, and squeezing me so that I felt like the meat in a sandwich. One farmer snored gently but by some miracle of gravity his evil-smelling pipe stuck to his lip. We bumped and scrunched past hedges to the main road and stopped at the bottom of a mountain and waited. A woman appeared. Another lemonade box came out, and the very large lady sat in front of me, our knees touching. She was holding a parcel. I could just see her face above it.

"We're not coming back that way."

"I don't think I'd make it."

We didn't! We were sitting comfortably in a seat when the others came back laden with goods bought in the market.

"Good job your mother isn't with us. She'd have made us come back the same way."

"Yes, she didn't like to offend the natives. It was always, *Do what they do*" But *we* weren't worried about it.

One day Les went fishing. Mrs Owen took Marion and me to visit a relative of hers on the other side of the mountain. On the way we saw a hen sitting in the hedge. Meir chased the bird away and took the egg it had laid.

"Do they often do that?" Marion wanted to know.

"Yes, many a time."

The hen was protesting loudly. We could hear it from miles away in the still air.

"Now we know how she has eggs to spare," Les said when I told him.

Inspite of everything, we enjoyed the holiday.

In September our road had their Victory party. It was probably much like all the others across the country. The thing I remember most about it was the pound of Madeira cake without coupons which the bread-man assured me was 'all butter'. We'd cut it into shapes and decorated for the party. I also remember the three-legged race for mothers in which one pair fell over.

Willing hands had carried our heavy piano out onto the street, but when it came to carrying it in again, they'd all disappeared. George (Elsie's husband) and Leslie had to struggle in with it by themselves. Never again, I vowed, would I let that happen.

But fate hadn't finished with me yet, there was more to come.

· Chapter Eleven ·

After all the excitement and celebrations for the ending of the war had died down, I thought we'd be able to settle down to our own lives. But no. It wasn't to be.

Edie came regularly to see me. One day she was ill and I had to go home with her.

"See you tomorrow," I said as I left.

I'd been trying to persuade Edie to do something about her daughter Barbara. "She's short-sighted."

"No, she's just clumsy. I know she bumps into us and falls over things."

"Haven't you noticed how closely she looks at anything, holding it right up to her eyes?"

"Don't interfere," Leslie said.

When I went to see Edie she was very ill, and had to have the doctor to see her. It was pleurisy!

As I was seeing the doctor out, I told him about the child.

"If what you say is true, she needs to see a specialist."

Edie was living over the butcher's shop that Tommy managed. She had two Irish terriers in the yard. They were tied up in the daytime. Although she was so small, it was Barbara who fed them. She had no fear of them. Nor of any animals. She was the one who calmed the dogs to let me past.

Edie had recovered from the illness, so I told her that

I'd asked the doctor about Barbara. She still didn't want to believe there was anything wrong.

"She's not wearing glasses," she declared.

"She'll have to when she goes to school."

We left it at that. I'd done my best for the child.

A few weeks later at nine o'clock one night there was a loud knocking on the door. It was Edie with Barbara.

"We've been thrown out of the flat."

"Where's Tommy and Peter?"

"Tommy's in a hostel run by the Corporation for homeless men. And Peter's with his Grandma."

We managed that night to put them up. Next day Edie went for a bed and a cot from the place where they'd stored their furniture. The single bed went into the back room where Marion slept. The cot had to go on the landing.

It wasn't too bad with Edie there, except that not much work was done. After a meal we'd sit at the table for half-an-hour while she smoked a cigarette. Leslie smoked as well. At night we'd play cards or darts with the room full of smoke.

Money was very scarce. Edie used to meet her husband to get some but it wasn't very much and sometimes we'd be searching our handbags and pockets to find a penny towards a loaf. As Leslie was working overtime to pay for furniture, I wouldn't ask him for any more, but once again juggled the money for the bills from one to another. I began to wonder if there'd ever come a time when I'd be able to simply pay the bills without having to steal from this one to pay that one.

After one of her meetings with her husband, Edie came back with Peter. "He wants to be with me."

I felt sorry for the boy left by himself. We now had to empty the boxroom into the cock-loft and put Marion in there. And find another bed to put in the other room for Peter. This was really getting too much for us.

Tommy didn't seem to be doing anything about finding a place for them. Edie herself had only made a few half-hearted attempts. Without success.

So who else could do something? Me. As usual!

"We'll go and see Mrs Braddock."

Mrs Braddock had a wonderful reputation for helping people who were homeless. The Corporation were building houses and flats. It had been impossible for Edie to even get her name on the housing list, they were in such demand.

"See your MP," somebody had suggested. But Edie was reluctant about going. So, as usual, it was left to me to take action. Our childhood roles had reversed. Now I was in the driver's seat!

"We're going to go and see Mrs Braddock," I said firmly.

Saturday was the day she gave interviews. The place was crowded when we arrived. She soon came bustling in.

"I can't see anyone who isn't in my constituency," she announced.

Edie got up to go.

"Sit down," I said. "We're not going, not after coming all this way."

I explained the situation to Mrs Braddock, and told her that my family had paid rates in Liverpool for generations. She agreed to listen to us.

"We bought a house when we married to make a better life for ourselves, but now with my sister and her children it's so crowded we can hardly move."

I told her about the cot on the landing and how there was scarcely space to move around. She was very sympathetic, realising that we were genuine. Edie only spoke once, when Mrs Braddock said, "I'll see what I can do for you. Where would you go?"

"Anywhere."

Well, she did do something. While we were waiting to hear, there was Barbara to see to. Edie got her an appointment for St Paul's Eye Hospital. Of course, I had to go with her and take Barbara in to see the specialist. After he'd examined her, he asked, "Does this child run about and play like other children?"

"Yes."

"You amaze me. She should have come sooner than this."

"I'm not her mother," I explained. "I'm her aunt."

So Barbara received spectacles.

When the notice came offering Edie a house, I was over-joyed. "You're going to take it?"

"Yes."

"Thank God for that!" I told Leslie. "I don't care who it is, we're not taking anybody else in. Not ever."

· Chapter Twelve ·

Tommy had managed to find a job at Napiers. It wasn't far from the new flat, which was the best place they'd had since they'd been married, he and Edie.

I was trying to sort myself out over the money. The rates hadn't been paid and we received a summons delivered by 'the Man in Black'. I knew he'd been to others in the road. His distinctive trilby hat and long black coat made him a dreaded figure. Remembering his mother's advice, "Don't tell your husband anything," I didn't tell Leslie. I did tell her however and she lent me the money. It was soon paid back now that Edie had gone. The council were very keen in those days only allowing a couple of weeks grace with payments.

Once again we had to try to live our own lives without (we hoped) disturbance. I'd like to say how wonderful it was, marriage, but it took a long time for us to adapt, and a great deal of worry. We had very different natures, Leslie and I. He was quite happy to sit with his feet up on the fireplace.

"You're taking all the polish off it," I'd complain.

Of course this was the winter I'm talking about. In the summer he worked in the garden. He took cuttings and found that it wasn't necessary to graft roses. When the roses and other flowers died in a vase, he discovered that splitting the stems when they were first cut prolonged their life. Everybody knows these things now, but we had to discover them for ourselves. I experimented with pot plants and friends still come to me for help and advice with their failures. We always listened to the gardening programmes on the wireless.

I still didn't know much about sex. It was a duty, a wife's duty. People didn't talk about it. At forty I thought I was starting the change, as we used to call the menopause, when in fact I was pregnant again.

The idea that I had to go through all that again terrified me. The first time, in the hospital with Marion, when anyone asked me, I'd always said I was fine. But this time I'd tell them. I really felt terrible about the whole prospect, but what did it matter? I was going to die anyway. Sleep was a small part of the night. The rest of it was spent in the bathroom to avoid waking Leslie. The song Wild Goose was popular then,and the words were running through my mind:

My heart knows where the wild goose goes

And I must go where the wild goose goes.

Friends would say, "The new baby, he'll be a comfort in your old age."

"I'm old already, too old for another baby."

"How d'ye know it'll be a boy?"

"I just know."

Hilda's husband had been very ill. Answering the door to her young daughter one day, she thrust a parcel into my hand saying, 'Me Dad's dead and can you use these sausages?'

Months later when I started with the pains, Leslie called at Hilda's on his way to work to ask her to go with me. After a day in the hospital my blood was counted again. It was only half the count it should have been. In those days doctors gave the blood transfusions. I felt very guilty he couldn't find a vein. He stuck the needle somewhere and it wasn't going in, so I told him. He said, "Mind your own business." It wasn't done, speaking to the doctor. The patient was only supposed to speak to the sister. The doctors usually stood well away from the bed so that the patient couldn't overhear what was being said.

Leslie was horrified when he saw my arm black and blue from elbow to wrist. "What have they been doing to you?"

"Only giving me a blood transfusion. The doctor told the sister I would die if I lost any more blood."

"How d'ye feel now?"

"Wonderful. I'll be home tomorrow."

Two days later the pains started. As Leslie couldn't stay away from work Hilda had promised to go with me.

Leslie was still working on the ships and was often laid off when one job was finished so he couldn't afford to lose any work. No matter what happened I always got my housekeeping money.

That day, he called at Hilda's on his way to tell her I was in labour and she rang for an ambulance. We were in the hospital by nine o'clock and I sat with several others outside the labour ward till two o'clock. The others were mostly young and scared. I was scared too. I felt like a grandmother trying to reassure them they'd be all right.

People used to say, "You soon forget." But not with a

memory like mine you don't. I can't believe how things have changed in child birth procedures. We went like lambs to the slaughter.

In hospitals in those days they did what they thought was right. Patients had no say in the treatment. I was dreading the thought of injections. I'd had fifty when Marion was born. Fifty! But it was all right. It seemed they'd given up that treatment, and used injections sparingly.

It <u>was</u> a boy. And inspite of my fears I survived to tell the tale though they kept me in a long time, long after the others who had come in with me had gone home with their babies. Even the woman who was older than me was allowed home, the one who had given birth at that age to her first baby, a 13lb son whom she called Vivian.

One girl was in disgrace. She wasn't married. She'd been told to wear a wedding ring to save trouble. I don't know where it would have come from. One of the patients or one of the staff. The poor girl would probably have to have the baby adopted.

"You haven't had an easy time," the sister said when she saw I was upset at being kept in hospital. "Just a few days longer."

A student had been visiting me every day and wanting to know what I was going to call the baby., but I couldn't decide. "I want something that can't be shortened."

Even when I was on my way out of the ward and home at last, she called out to me, but I just said "No!"

It was a surprise to see Elsie had come to fetch me.

"Hilda had an appointment today," she said. "She asked me to come for you."

Elsie and I had fallen out since a woman called Peggy who had moved into the street had come between us. I didn't like Peggy. Elsie was a generous person and this Peggy was taking advantage of her. Peggy's husband was still at home while George, Elsie's husband, was away fighting. I'd dropped out and left them to it.

By collecting me from the hospital, Elsie had offered me an olive branch and I was pleased about it. Elsie and I were getting friendly again.

· Chapter Thirteen ·

At home Elsie settled us down. We had no coal. With nobody in the house the men hadn't left any. We had a portable gas fire which wasn't very reliable. Elsie went over to her house and brought some coal and lit the fire, and made a cup of tea.

"The coalman should be here tomorrow. We can return it then," I told her before she left. It felt good that we were on friendly terms again.

Leslie came home early. The child was screaming. He was hungry and there was no food for him. He'd been given a bottle before we'd left the hospital.

Starting all over again after twelve years was expensive. It meant buying a cot, a pram and other essentials. I didn't think we'd need a bottle. With Marion, I'd supplied the whole ward with milk. This time I had none. Leslie dashed out to the Chemist, coming back with a bottle and baby food, and the child was soon asleep. Marion helped to make a meal and when we'd dined I went to bed with the baby.

I felt happy and smug. I'd come out of it well with this lovely child snuggling up to me. I was fast asleep when my husband came up to put the baby in his cot.

It was hard going, getting back into a routine, waking in the night, washing nappies. Leslie helped a lot but ingrained into him was the idea of 'women's work' which a man (a self-respecting man) would be ashamed to be seen doing. Washing dishes was definitely women's work, though I have to admit he didn't mind making his own breakfast and bringing me up a cup of tea every morning.

We'd had the baby christened Eric and William after his Grandad. I'd thought Eric was a name that couldn't be shortened, but I was wrong. As he grew up his school mates called Ike which they still do today.

Eric slept in a cot beside the bed and when he cried at night I'd lean over and stuff a dummy into his mouth. This wasn't enough for him, so I'd dip the dummy in a jar of Virol from the clinic which was supposed 'to keep the baby healthy'. In the morning there was usually Virol all over his face where I'd missed his mouth, poor little chap. Virol was fawn-coloured so Eric looked dreadful, plastered in the stuff, so I changed to condensed milk, the best of course, and that didn't look so bad.

Eric was very different from Marion. She could always be persuaded to do what I wanted her to. But not Eric. From the start he was a very determined young man.

"He takes after you," Leslie said.

It turned out to be a battle of wills.

One particular day it was freezing and he wanted to play out. A neighbour who was a dressmaker had made him a coat but he'd taken a dislike to it and wouldn't have it on. We fought all day.

"You're not going out without your coat," I told him. But every time anyone knocked at the door the child would try to escape.

"Let him go out," Elsie said when she came over. "He won't come to any harm."

"I'm the boss here," I said.

That was only one of several occasions. There was the night when he wouldn't come in from play, so I locked the door on him. "You can stay out all night then." Eventually he knocked on the door and I thought I'd won, but no!

"I'm not comin' in," he explained. "I've come back for me bike."

My mother-in-law took us both to the Isle of Man for a holiday with her sister-in-law, Aunty Olive. I knew Aunty Olive from our Boxing Day visits years before when all the family gathered together. If the weather was bad, we'd stay the night. In those far away days she'd give us all a dose of cough mixture at bedtime. Now on arrival at the boarding house on the Isle of Man I was amazed at the supply of medicines she unpacked.

"She always takes them wherever she goes," Leslie's mother told me.

There was cough mixture, aspirins, indigestion tablets, Wintergreen oil for rubbing, bandages and even a small bottle of Brandy.

"She's a hypochondriac," I said, showing off my vocabulary.

"What's that?"

"People who think they're always ill."

"That's Aunty Olive all right."

Our lodgings were at the top of a hill and toiling back up it after a day on the beach, Aunty Olive offered to push the go-chair.

At the top she said, "It's cured my indigestion."

"Well," I said, "you can do that every night." Which she did.

Eric hadn't been too bad. He never was when we were out. That is, until we were in the queue for the boat home. A lady in front of us was wearing a mac exactly like mine. Mine was in the suitcase.

"That's your mac!" he shouted, and despite trying to explain to him that mine was in the case, he wouldn't believe it. The case had to be opened so that he could see the mac for himself.

He was the same at home. When Edie visited she'd always have her shopping bag with her. Before she left, she'd have to empty it out in case she was running off with something belonging to Eric.

He hated going to bed and resented the idea that Marion was staying up later than him. We had a budgie which kept saying, "Go to bed Eric." He blamed Marion for any trouble he was in. Once he carved a capital **E** on the back of 'his' chair. "Marion did it," he said.

In the mean time, my sense of well-being was gradually fading away. Every time I had a cough I was sent for an X-ray, sometime to this hospital, sometimes to that. And inspite of all the doctor's efforts, I was still losing blood as fast as they could give me transfusions. Things went on like this (though I don't think the doctor believed me) until 1953 when I ended up in hospital again.

"I'm afraid you have a fistula," they told me.

My heart sank. It was a fistula that killed my brother Alf. But fortunately there had been big advances in medicine since then and things worked out better for me.

Broadgreen Hospital had changed from a TB Sanitorium to an ordinary general hospital. A block of wards had been built during the war to house wounded soldiers. They were known as A1, A2 and so on. I was in Ward N2 which the nurses called 'Nellie'. It was a long narrow ward with 24 beds in it. The Sister's office had a window in it from which whoever was on duty could keep an eagle eye on us all. A table in the centre held all the flowers which were removed from the ward at night and brought back in the morning. Nothing was ever allowed to be left on our lockers. The doctors came round every morning to see us all lying there washed and brushed and tucked tightly into our immaculate beds with not so much as a crease in a counterpane.

While I was in hospital, Elsie had promised to look after Eric during the day. Between them, Leslie and Marion were able to manage the cooking and the housework, although she was doing her O Level exams that summer.

When they came to visit me at Broadgreen, I asked how everything was going.

"We're doing all right," Leslie said. "She buys mincemeat and it lasts all week because she keeps adding water to it."

"Is Eric all right?"

In those days, children weren't allowed to visit people in hospital. And only two visitors were allowed at once. There was no visiting at all on Wednesday nights when the nurses gave the ward a good clean. As I've said, nothing was ever left out on top of our lockers, and we were definitely not allowed to sit on our beds. The main

Portrait taken shortly before I was married.

Leslie

Studio photographs were very popular

Meeting Leslie's relatives at Ross on Sea

Marion at 3 months

Marian in the pram I had to push

Eric on the second motor cycle

Sister Edie and friend Elsie

My first dressmaking attempt

Marions wedding

Evelyn and me with the hats we made for Marion's wedding

Golden Wedding

thing was to have the place looking tidy, no matter how uncomfortable it was.

"Well," Marion said, "I took Eric to Sunday School. Dad put his coat on for him and as soon as we got outside he flung it off. And he walked on the backs of his shoes both there and back."

"But you're not to worry – we're doing all right."

"So you're not missing me?"

"Of course we are. The hospital have told us not to keep ringing in all the time."

It was a surgical ward, N2, with mostly cancer patients and poor souls in the last stages of TB. In comparison, my problems didn't seem too bad.

After three months and three operations I was told I could go home. To my disappointment, when Leslie came to visit me and heard the news, he said "Oh no!"

"Don't you want me home, then?"

"Of course I do."

"It doesn't sound like it."

Leslie didn't have much tact and always uttered his first thought.

Elsie came to fetch me with Eric, but I'd been laid up in hospital so long that he didn't know me and clung on to Elsi's hand.

"He's not the only one who doesn't want me back," I told her.

"I know," she said. "Leslie came to me in a panic about the state of the house. Marion and I were working till three o'clock this morning to clean it."

So everything would be all right. My Guardian Angel hadn't deserted me after all.

· Chapter Fourteen ·

Once back home it was very difficult to get back into a routine again, although I had been helping the nurses to make beds and do the flowers on the ward which were real chores for them. They were glad to have someone to arrange the flowers for the patients. We didn't get a cup of tea after lunch, so one nurse I was friendly with used to say, "Help me with the beds and I'll make you an oesophagus soother."

But it was a matter of taking over the reins at home again, winning Eric's confidence and generally coping. It wasn't easy, the two years before Eric went to school. There were arguments if I complained about anything.

Leslie would say, "Don't nag."

He was quite content to stay at home. Marion and I sometimes went out, but she had her own friends. She had obtained six O Levels which was very good considering all the strain she'd been under. I was very proud of her.

"I don't want to stay at school," she said. "I'll get a job."

"Did you want her to stay on?" her father asked.

"It's not what I want. If she'd rather leave, that's it."

She soon found a place in the library.

What a wonderful job, I thought. All those books.

Plenty of friends came to visit us. Always my friends, mind.

Ella had married Tom, the man she'd originally turned down because he was a sailor. He'd given up the sea and now worked at BAT. They had one child and Ella fussed over him like a mother hen with one chick. It was, "Let me fasten your coat up Brien, you'll get cold."

And I thought of my children. Who would come off best in the hard world that was waiting for them out there?

Ella lived in the same house she was born in and never moved anywhere else. She died there too.

Margery, another friend from school days, had come to live in the neighbourhood. We met often, but always during the daytime as most women had to stay at home in the evening to look after their children. Margery was a very clever dressmaker and did alterations at home to supplement her husband's wages. We have always kept in touch, Margery and I, and still meet occasionally. Although it can be a long time in between, when we do get together nowadays it is as though it were yesterday, these days I'm writing of when we were young and both busy with children of our own.

Lily, my other friend from school and from work, was a frequent visitor too. After she'd been discharged from the Sanatorium, she'd gone back to work until she left to look after her parents. She was with them until they died. Later, she married Ted, a man she'd met in the Sanatorium. His only relative was a sister who wasn't pleased when he married. Lily was a wonderful person – everybody liked her. She was always jolly and had a fund of jokes both clean and smutty which she'd tell according to the company she happened to be in. She swore a lot but wouldn't allow me to even say 'damn'.

"I'll do all the swearing round here," she'd say.

Her husband had been ill for a while. When he wrote out a will on a piece of scrap paper, I witnessed it. After he died, I was ordered to see the Probate Officer. He was a very stern imposing man. Eric was with me. The man spoke to him but Eric just kept staring and then said in a loud clear voice, "Big 'ead!"

"It's a song on the radio," I explained apologetically.

"That's all right," he said. "I've had worse things than that said to me."

After the troopships were repaired from the ravages of war and refurbished in preparation for cruises, work slackened off and the men were finished too. The men went to different shipping lines for work. The pay was very good, but in between jobs there wasn't any. Leslie was never out of work for very long because the firms soon found out who the best workers were. When he was working Leslie always saved as much as he could. I never knew how much he earned and didn't care – he always made sure I had my housekeeping money.

Leslie spent his spare time improving the house, making cupboards that were soon filled. The only trouble was that at work he had a labourer to do the menial chores. You can guess who filled the labourer's role at home! He had fixed ideas about what should be done and how it should be done and no amount of argument could change them.

"Don't grumble," he'd say, and I'd remember a song we learnt at school.

Oh don't the days seem lank and long
When everything's right and nothing's wrong.
And wouldn't life seem dreadfully flat
When there's nothing at all to grumble at.

With a few set-backs and visits to hospitals I was gradually getting back to normal. With plenty of friends and my Mother-in-law who was very good to me, buying clothes for Eric, we managed all right but it wasn't easy, especially when unexpected expenses came along.

It was time for Eric to go to school and of course he didn't want to go. He'd rather play out. I'd found out that Eric was like me. He'd be led but not driven.

"Everybody has to go to school," I told him, "so make up your mind which one to go to."

We chose Park View where some of his mates went.

After the first day, he said, "I don't want you to come with me." so we arranged that one of the older girls who lived in the road would call for him. Every morning he found a reason for not going.

"I feel sick." "I've got a headache."

It was no use forcing him, so I'd say to him, "Tell the teacher if you don't feel well and she'll find someone to bring you home."

He never came home until school was over. One time he had a cyst in his eye and had to go to hospital.

"It's easier without an anaesthetic," he was told.

It might have been easier for the doctor but it was painful for Eric but he never murmured.

He wasn't doing so well with his reading, and talking to some of the other mothers I realised that they weren't happy with the teaching either. A visit to the headmaster gave me no satisfaction so I decided to pay for Eric to have some private tuition. Leslie promised that he'd find the money. It was only an hour a week but every Tuesday Eric protested about having to go.

"If you want to be a labourer, that's all right by me," I told him. But it made no difference to Eric's attitude. Eventually I told his Dad the protests he was making.

Leslie said, "I'll talk to him."

Apparently all he said to the child was this: "Don't bother going son. I'll put in a word for you at the Docks."

From then on we had no more trouble with him. He worked hard at school and at the tutor's.

· Chapter Fifteen ·

Our friends Tom and Mary who lived over the road had relations in Oswaldtwistle. One day when Mary was visiting them she invited us to go with her. This was before Eric had started school.

Mary's uncle was a huge man with an enormous appetite. I was amazed at the amount of food he ate, dinner and bilberry pie afterwards. A couple of years later he died. Tom and Mary moved there to look after the shop. I took Eric with me for the weekend. Eric was playing with Mary's children when there was an accident. One of them had swung him round by his feet and banged his head on the kerb. It looked awful. We took him to a doctor who said, "It's not as bad as it looks." I dreaded going home, knowing I'd get, "Why weren't you watching him?" And, "You'd better not go again." But my Mother-in-law was there when we got home and as soon as she saw Leslie opening his mouth to speak she said, "Don't say anything." And he didn't. Not even after she'd gone. I went again for weekends for any happy events.

Tom did trade contests. I did too. But all the years we did them we only received consolation prizes, both of us.

Later they moved to Accrington to run their own shop. On our first visit there it was quite an experience finding how to reach our destination outside the town. The Lancashire people are so friendly, I'd just ask in the bus the way Mary told me to, and all the people on board would work out the best route, arguing among themselves, saying "No, don't go that way, this way's nearer."

I'd serve in the shop sometimes if Mary was busy elsewhere and as often as not I'd have to say to the customer, "Excuse me a minute," and slip out and ask, "What does she want?"

As the children grew up they had independent holidays, Marion going with her friends, Eric going to camp with the Boys Brigade.

Elsie and I decided to go to Night School. It was free in those days. We went to Dressmaking. We both had sewing machines. Mine was Queenie's old treadle. I hadn't seen Queenie for years. She'd gone back to our old neighbourhood. Edie met her once. Now I was able to make dresses for Marion and myself, which was a saving.

After Dressmaking we went to Soft Furnishing classes. I made three eiderdowns, two cushions in Italian quilting and numerous lampshades with fringes.

Elsie didn't want to go to the Typing class so I went alone. I didn't take it seriously as I thought I'd only ever need typing for the letters I sent to magazines. When payment for my contributions started coming in Leslie always had material for me to write about, tales of the dockers. If a ship had to be fitted quickly there was overtime to be had. He used to suggest the names of the men should be put in a hat to see who would get the overtime. So his fellow-joiners began to call him 'the Magician'.

"Have you heard the name they've given to Joe?" one of the men said. "They call him the Good Shepherd."

"Why?"

"He managed to get away with a whole lamb." A frozen lamb carcass off one of the refrigerator ships they were unloading from New Zealand.

"That's nothing. How about the feller with the one arm? He filled his empty sleeve with bars of chocolate."

"You should write that down and send it somewhere."

"How about me writing about the time you went to Blackpool on the firm's picnic."

It seemed they all joined a club and had to sign in. "Well," he said, "I was amazed when all the names were Jones. I wasn't going to be the only one to put down the right name so I signed myself Smith. By the way, I need a hair-cut."

Something else I did, I cut everyone's hair, my own included. Until the children decided they'd rather have a professional to do it. But I went on cutting Leslie's for a long time. One day I nicked his ear. "That's it," he said. "No more. You might take a piece out of my ear next time. Your hand trembles too much nowadays."

Though I lost that job, there were plenty more for me to do, such as writing a letter of complaint.

"You do it better than I can," my neice Edie said. "I've sent three but got no reply from any of them."

She was writing to a tobacco company that wouldn't honour the coupons she'd collected. So I wrote, finishing the letter: "If you think we smoke ourselves to death for you to do us out of the things we want . . ."

A parcel was delivered the next week. From then on, others would ask me to do the same for them, write letters of complaint or whatever.

People were prospering and buying new goods. Shops

were investing in fridges and radios, all very different from the ones we had already. Much more stylish.

The first person to own a television was Gladys and she would invite some of the neighbours in to watch any special programmes. We'd crowd into the small living-room. The light was put out to get a better picture. How wonderful we thought it was! A bit of a change from play-ing darts. The first time we went to watch Gladys's telly, it was teeming with rain so that the sound had to be turned right up against the competition. When ITV started we got a television too. Eric pestered until we did. It wasn't a success. The picture was always rolling with somebody jumping up to adjust it. It was a relief when we got rid of that first set.

The Electricity often broke down. Sometimes I was just cooking the dinner when it went off. Then it was back to candles. If it went off in the daytime, the fridges in the shops gave up and the rumour came round, "They're selling off the food cheaply. Before it goes off." We'd go down to get our share from whichever shop it was. Prices had risen on most things, but the wage increases had to be fought for.

My friend Lily was living in lodgings with a lady she thought was her friend, but it wasn't working out.

"You'll have to see a councillor," I told her.

"I will if you come with me."

So Sunday mornings, for over six months, we went to see him and eventually she was given a bed-sitter in Kirkby.

· Chapter Sixteen ·

I had heard through the 'Bush Telegraph' that Queenie was back in the neighbourhood, so I decided to visit her. The two boys, Alfie and Arthur were there.

"You come to wash us?"

"No, I think you can manage it yourselves now you're married."

As well as the two sons, there was Edie, another daughter whom I hadn't met before, and Sam her husband.

"How's Dot? I heard she was married."

"Yes. She's got seven children."

"D'ye ever see Dolly?"

"No!" And I thought how foolish Dolly was to be missing all this, having nothing to do with any of us.

Edie and Sam had a caravan in Leasowe and Queenie often stayed there by herself. I'd go for a day sometimes.

"Can't you come and stay for a few days?" Queenie asked me.

"You go," Leslie urged when it was mentioned. So I did. We had a great time catching up on all the things we'd been doing, each of us, knitting furiously as we talked. Unfortunately Queenie's knitting suffered.

"Can you do anything with this?"

It was a Fair Isle jumper she was knitting with a Dutch boy and girl. As we chattered away, she'd put the girl's head on the boy and vice versa. Her sight wasn't good but mine was so it was soon put right.

I really enjoyed my trips to the caravan especially when Edie joined us at the weekend. I grew very fond of Edie. I still am, after all these years. I think she's fond of me too.

One day my sister Edie and I went to visit Queenie. It was very pleasant until they started arguing over something trivial, shouting at one another.

"Stop it!" I said. "You sound like a couple of fishwives. I thought you'd given that sort of thing up." But evidently they hadn't changed.

Edie put her coat on. "You coming, Flo?"

"No I'm not."

I'd been fed up with their quarrelling before I was married and determined not to allow it in my own home. When Leslie and I argued it was never in front of the children. He always left it to me to scold or correct them and never interfered not even when he didn't agree with me over anything I'd said to them. He'd wait until we were alone to tell me. And even then it was soon all friendliness between us again.

One night when we were at Leslie's Mother's she was very upset over losing her cleaner, so I offered to do it and go over once a week and clean her house from top to bottom. Then Brenda, Arthur's wife, began to take a share which made it a lot easier, doing it between us.

Mrs Jones always loved a bargain. When Lewis's had a sale she'd pick up bargains like a card table with a broken leg, or chairs with legs missing. Having two joiners in the family, these items were easily mended. One time she bought a round table which wobbled every time anybody moved. It had a very short life!

She was Chairman of the Conservative Club. Every week she made tarts filled with either jam or lemon cheese for the refreshments. One week she said, "I think I'm going mad. I've forgotten to put the lemon cheese in." So we filled the tarts up and took them along to the meeting. The same thing happened the next week.

"Don't worry about it," I told her. "We all forget things."

I'd just arrived the next week, when the cat ran out of the sitting room where the tarts were left with one in its mouth and dropped it.

"I'm so relieved to find out what's been happening," my Mother-in-law said. "I thought my mind was going. Fancy the cat licking the lemon cheese out of them like that!" "Never mind, let's fill them up again. What the eye doesn't see the heart doesn't grieve over". "I'll make certain the door's shut in future."

I only went to the Conservative Club as an entertainer singing Gracie Fields songs, 'Sing as we go,' and 'The biggest aspidistra in the world.' The old ladies called me Gracie Fields.

Leslie didn't want to go out, not even to see his brothers. The only time we saw them was at Christmas or the odd weekend at his mother's. Then they'd only argue about football. If we were asked out, Leslie would say, "You go." Yet when he was persuaded to go anywhere he'd be the life and soul of the party.

One day I was repeating some of the gossip I'd heard

to him when he said, "D'ye remember that poem they taught us in school about the owl?"

"Yes."

A wise old owl sat on an oak.
The more he heard, the less he spoke.
The less he spoke, the more he heard.
Why can't we be like that wise old bird?

I took the hint!

Although he was friendly with everybody, it was only the mate Leslie worked with who used to visit. He'd stay for hours. He wouldn't have a meal with us and he wouldn't go. He drifted away once that particular job was finished.

Life seemed very dull. A day out with the old ladies. Knitting, sewing, crocheting. A new sewing machine didn't make much difference. I was only going through the motions.

Marion was courting by this time so we didn't go to the pictures any more, she and I. I was happy enough with plenty of friends and only a few illnesses.

Then one wonderful day I met someone who was to change my life completely.

· Chapter Seventeen ·

It was on the bus going to see Edie that I met a girl I recognised from work. She sat down beside me and said "Hello".

"I've seen you in the factory but I don't think we've spoken to one another."

"I've heard the boss calling you."

"That was if I was late, but he used to clock on for me."

"My name's Evelyn."

"I'm called Flo now."

And that's how the rest of my life started!

We talked about the factory. Evelyn hadn't liked it very much either. She told me what the boss used to call me: "A square peg in a round hole, that's Florence."

"I got married and stayed on for a while, but then the firm found out and I had to leave, although I could have done with the money."

"I have to get off here," I said. "I'll see you again."

And sure enough we did meet again, in one of the shops in Huyton village. Again, we talked for a while, and then she said,

"Would you like to come home with me, Flo? Have you got time today?"

We were soon sitting in her kitchen with a pot of tea.

"Where is it you're going when we meet on the bus?" I asked her.

"To the Trefoil Guild, one of their meetings."

"The Trefoil Guild! What's that then? I've never heard of it."

"I used to be in the Guides," I said. "In one of the first companies in Liverpool."

"Why don't you join the Trefoil Guild then?

"I don't think so. What do they do?"

"Oh, you know, everything to help their local Guide company. To raise money and that. It's fun. And it's useful. Why don't you come along to our next meeting and see what you think?"

"They may not like a stranger turning up."

"You lived up that way, didn't you. You might well know some of them."

So rather reluctantly I agreed to meet Evelyn before hand and go with her to the next meeting.

Her branch of the Trefoil Guild met in the different members' houses. This time it was at Winnie's.

"Are you sure it'll be all right?"

"Of course it will. You remember the Guide law, 'A Guide is a friend to all'. It will be fine."

And so it turned out to be. Some of them had known my family and we all had friends in common. Soon we were chatting away, sharing our childhood memories.

"Remember the day Princess Margaret visited the Guide headquarters?"

From 1920 ex-members of Girl Guide companies, wanting to keep in touch with friends they had made as Guides, formed groups which amalagamated under the name of "Old Guides". 1943 saw the appointment of a Recorder from headquarters and a change of name to "The Trefoil Guild".

"Oh, yes . . ."

"It poured down . . ."

"And we were all sloshing around the field in our wellington boots."

"Remember . . ."

When the laughter died down the Guild members got down to business. They were arranging something that they called A Pound Night, something I'd never heard of but they soon explained.

"We each bring along a pound of something – maybe a pound of jam, carrots, rice, whatever. Then we each buy one of the contributions the others have brought along."

Today this idea has blossomed into the Bring & Buy sale. But then it was a new idea. And nearly everyone could afford to give a pound of something, if it was only a pound of potatoes.

I thoroughly enjoyed that first Trefoil Guild meeting that Evelyn took me along to. At the next meeting I joined properly, repeating the Guide Promise first made so long before:

I promise on my honour to do my best to do my duty to God and the Queen, to help other people at all times, and to obey the Guide laws.

The Guide laws were very strict, encompassing everything that was good. They hadn't meant much to me as a child, but now it struck me that you'd have to be an angel to keep them all.

I was given a badge and welcomed into the company.

And joining the Trefoil Guild turned out to be the best thing I'd ever done.

There was so much going on in the Guild. The first thing was helping to run the library in Newsham Hospital. It was no longer 'the Workhouse' that it used to be. A couple of us used to go round the men's wards. One man always asked me to recommend which books he should take. Whether he ever read them was anybody's guess. One week when I wasn't there, the others said, "That fellah was asking where you were, Flo."

"He likes the books I choose for him."

"Oh, yes – that must be it." And they went away laughing.

The next week, when I went round with the library trolley, the man said, "I fancy you."

"Do you? So does somebody else, as it happens, my husband."

This went on for a few weeks. One day he said to me, "Would you leave your husband? Would you leave him for £500?"

"Not for a million."

When I told Leslie about it we had a good laugh.

"By the way," I said to him, "when the others heard about my admirer it started a discussion as to what their men had thought about them before they asked them out. What was it that attracted you to me?"

"You always looked so clean."

"That's not very romantic, Leslie."

"If you must know, it was love at first sight."

It certainly wasn't my money he was after because I simply didn't have any.

The romance in my life came with the cup of tea that Leslie brought me up to bed every morning. And the box of chocolates he'd always bring me on pay day. To say nothing of the bunch of flowers I'd get whenever he'd been fishing. So I guess I can't grumble.

There were some Trefoil Guild coach trips, and as we got to know different people and their different situations, perhaps sitting beside one of two sisters on the way there, and the other sister on the way back, discretion was called for.

These two sisters, for instance, shared a house. They had neither of them been married. One went out to work, the other kept house. The both seemed quite happy with this arrangement, until the working sister retired, that is.

"She interferes in the housework and wants to do the shopping," Joan said.

"I only want to help her," Mary said, "to do my whack."

This sort of argy-bargy went on in quite a few households, I was told.

We organised coach trips for our own company, and as I met more members of other groups at visits and conferences, more people invited me to their functions. Through the Trefoil Guild I made so many friends and learnt so many useful and interesting things – joining the organisation was certainly the best thing I've ever done.

Evelyn, who had introduced me to the Guild, became my best friend. We seemed to have so much in common, she and I. She had three sons, and she was as eager as I was to ensure that our children had a better life than we had had.

We were both interested in everything around, though our tastes in reading were different. She went to Night School and gained several O Levels. She was artistic, and showed me how to make bowls of cacti for presents. She was also very house-proud – her house was always sparkling (very different from my own, I'm afraid!). I was always amazed that with all those males living there, her husband and their three sons, she could keep the place so clean and tidy!

Now that I was a member of the Trefoil Guild, my life was so full and so busy. There were coffee mornings, Bring & Buys, meetings, outings, visits and visitors.

Inspite of all these new activities, the housework was not neglected, nor was my family. The dinner always had to be on the table the minute Leslie came in from work. He was a good husband, a good provider, and he worked hard, so a good meal waiting for him when he got home was little enough to ask in return.

Leslie loved his home. I loved it too. But I wasn't content to stay in it as much as he was. He looked after me and was good to me when I was ill, but he wasn't a fusser, Leslie. Sometimes I felt a bit resentful about that, especially when I heard how some men cosseted their wives when they were pregnant or poorly.

But now looking back I'm glad that things worked out they way they did. It was partly thanks to Leslie that I became both strong and self-reliant.

· Chapter Eighteen ·

Before Marion was engaged to Peter, he owned an Auto-Scooter. One night they were on their way to a Scooter club meeting when there was an accident and they were taken to hospital. Peter's parents were told, but we weren't. The first we heard was his parents calling on us, introducing themselves and telling us that they weren't badly hurt, the pair of them, and Marion would be coming home. We realised then that this relationship was going to be serious. I had the feeling that Peter's parents didn't really approve of us. They felt superior.

After all, Leslie was only a City and Guilds joiner, while I was an ex-factory worker. They owned a shop.

Marion had left the library to work in the Imperial Chemical Industry in the Liver Building in Liverpool. Eventually ICI moved to Runcorn, but when they fixed the wedding date, it was too far away, so she left there and started in the Housing Department of Liverpool Corporation. They were buying a new house in Easham on the other side of the river, and as she intended to carry on working it was nearer the tunnel for them to go to work.

The wedding was a huge success with all the trimmings, the breakfast, then the band at night. I don't claim all the kudos for it, the fact that we weren't drinkers ourselves and ordered too much really helped it to go with a swing. Some people still remember Marion's wedding!

Afterwards, the house was very quiet without her. We missed her stories of the reasons some give for their preference for a house on this estate or that. Some of the new estates were given nick-names. One woman who was offered a certain place said, "I will not go on the Panda Rosa." These sorts of things Marion always remembered.

Eric was out most nights. In the winter I'd put an electric blanket in his bed. One night, he woke me as he came in. There was a smell of smoke. I went into his room to see the bed on fire with flames rising to the ceiling. Shouting to the other two to bring a bucket of water, I grabbed some towels, soaked them in it and put the fire out. One half of the bed was burned right through. It was my fault. I'd left the control switch on the bed. It had shorted and started the fire.

"You should never do that," they said.

"Anyway, it was me that put it out."

For the time being, all the bed-clothes were put in the out-house including a feather eiderdown. Next morning when the door was opened, the wind blew the feathers all over the house – burnt or charred feathers!

Evelyn had been taking the minutes of the executive meetings of the RNIB and she asked me to go along with her. Both for company and to take over if she couldn't go any time. Before long we were helping at the Blind School, and fund-raising for them. Some of the wives of the RNIB committee members organised fund-raising functions in their own homes, especially the rich ones. We sensed the same sort of attitude to us as if we were being paid, which of course we weren't. We were volunteers the same as them, even though we were ordinary working-class women. They couldn't stomach that, the RNIB 'ladies'!

Once a year, the week they had a collection for the blind, Evelyn and I also went to the Liverpool football ground to count the money that had been given. The first time, I met the groundsman who said, "I remember you – you haven't changed since we went to school."

"Well I hope I didn't look like this in my school days."

On one occasion I met the photographer from The Echo who said, "You know my sister." We talked about what we'd been doing since we left school. His sister had married a butcher. Then he went off to take pictures of the game.

To start with there was only one lady on the committee of the RNIB. She was with her husband. They were both blind. Later another lady joined them, she always had plenty to say. She told us that inspite of being blind, she was a writer and that she was hoping to find someone who would read for her. She wrote short stories for magazines but didn't know what kind they accepted since she could no longer read them for herself. "I just need somebody to come and read to me, one night a week would do."

I should have had more sense, but fell into the trap and offered to be her reader. She was very exacting and if I wasn't there right on time she'd say, "You're late."

"It was teeming with rain," I remember telling her once, "so I waited for it to go off a bit."

"You're not sugar. You won't melt."

"It's not as heavy here, our way it was pouring."

"Well it must stop somewhere. What time do you have to go?"

It didn't matter what time I told her, she'd always keep me longer. As often as not, on my way out she'd hand me a bundle of tape from the recorder. "Sort these out before you go." And I'd be waiting for the last bus. She never offered to pay for a taxi and I certainly couldn't afford one.

After a while in addition to reading to her she gave me the job of going over her scripts. They were very old-fashioned. Even then I could see she'd been sending them to the wrong type of magazine. Even contributions to the Readers' Letters Page had to be sent to the right market.

"My friends say my work is very good," she told me.

"You shouldn't take any notice of friends," I said. "They're obviously biased."

I started to read her magazine stories out loud to her. I corrected them, she'd type them out and we'd get them posted. But her efforts were all rejected, they were all coming back!

She told me she'd joined a Writers' Club.

One night, waiting for last bus (as usual) on a main road with nobody else about, a man who seemed to come from nowhere walked up to me.

"Waiting for a bus?"

"Obviously."

"I have a motorbike. Can I give you a lift home?"

"Why?"

"You're a nice young lady to be waiting on your own."

"I'm not young. I have a son older than you." And to my relief the bus appeared. "Thanks very much – here's the bus now."

Having to be up at five in the morning, Leslie always went to bed early. After he'd heard about this incident he said, "I think you'd be better going over there in the daytime." Which I did. But that was a mistake too. We went shopping for her. She lived in a flat and while I was involved with her she moved twice, making sure that the move was on *my* day. I'll never know how I managed, pushing furniture around for her, laying carpets and all.

Because she was blind she often got free tickets and took me with her to Police concerts, plays, theatre and even a boat trip to Llandudno. All free. Because I didn't like the idea of her by herself all weekend in a miserable flat, she began spending Bank Holidays at our house. On one of these visits I got very annoyed with her.

"Your underskirt is showing," she said.

I went upstairs to fix it.

When I came down she said, "It's still showing."

"I thought you were blind."

"Partially sighted."

I went and made the tea.

· Chapter Nineteen ·

Occasionally Evelyn and I went to the Consumer Council tasting food and testing products for the big producers. One time I remember I was called in after Evelyn and was surprised to see her on her knees scrubbing the floor.

"What'ye doin'?"

"She asked me how I cleaned the floor."

"She asked me as well but I told her I use a mop."

We'd also joined the Vigilance Society and were on the committee. This was a charity to help travellers who came into Liverpool. One woman would meet the early ships and help people to find the bus or train to take them on the next leg of their journey. Another woman met early trains and saw passengers to their ship or whatever. These two had to be admired for their dedication in turning out at the crack of dawn in all sorts of weather, summer and winter. When the Society had the usual fund-raising day, apart from the gifts that had been donated by the big shops, the goods that were put out for sale often looked tired, old and shabby.

"They're left over from last year," the secretary explained.

"Do you always do that?"

"People who've given them will recognise their stuff and won't bother giving anything else."

The answer was to put the prices down – then everything was sold.

"That's good," the secretary said. "That will save me taking them home again. That's what I've always had to do. Mrs Thingummy would never let us reduce the prices."

"If she complains, just tell her to come to see us," I said. But we heard no more about it. Maybe she was scared of us, Mrs Thingummy!

"She always wants to be the Chairman," someone explained.

"Yes, and at the meetings she'd go on and on . . . "

"We'd never get home . . . "

Evelyn left after a while, but I stayed on until the organisation had to be disbanded – the money wasn't coming in, and most of the travellers were pregnant girls from Ireland seeking abortions, and taking advantage of the hospitality of the people who felt responsible for them. The secretary herself took one of these girls in and told us, "I thought she'd never go."

One of the women from the Consumer Council called and asked if she could come and see how I did the washing.

"Why?"

"Because you don't have a washing machine, do you."

"I do. It's on two legs. I'm the washing machine in our house!"

The woman came and was surprised at the results I got washing by hand. She gave me a small prize and probably boosted the powder I used.

The years were flying by and many things had happened.

Leslie had gone through the whole range of transport from a cycle to a small motorbike, a larger one, one with a side-car and on to a Reliant three-wheeler car.

Marion had left work when she was pregnant with her son. He was two years old when she and Peter decided to leave the wilds of Wirral and come back to Roby.

My sister-in-law Olive died of heart disease at 40. I grew very close to my mother-in-law, Mrs Jones, at that time.

Eric had passed his exams and was working in an office with Peter.

Although Evelyn and I didn't see as much of each other, we still were together at meetings and on Trefoil Guild outings.

Talking to a lady who'd moved from our road, she told me how she was missing her daughter who was married and living abroad. I asked her to come to the Trefoil Guild. She did, and brought a friend with her, Stella. We liked one another immediately, Stella and I, and soon we were visiting each other and comparing notes about writing. She wrote poetry and I showed her the letters of mine that had been published. This was the start of a new phase in my life.

Stella started going with me to the blind woman who was getting more exacting. She'd keep us so late that we were often mixed up in the rush-hour traffic making us too late to get home and cook a meal. One day we were extra late leaving because as we were ready to go she fainted and then we couldn't leave her until the doctor arrived.

He said, "She'll be all right, she's a tough old bird."

"Do you think we should ring her daughter "' Stella said.

"No. She doesn't want to trouble her daughter. She always relies on me. Leslie thinks it's time I gave up."

"When you think about it, we're helping her so much nowadays that we're practically writing her stories."

When we told her, she was all right about it.

Stella and I decided to join the Writers Club. We sat at the back. Our blind friend sat at the front and always had plenty to say. She even persuaded a man to take her home in his car. Afterwards he told us he always had to go in and switch the lights on for her.

I extended my letters into articles, and kept on with both. Money from published letters was a help in paying for the postage on articles which at that time just kept coming back, rejected.

Stella was more successful. She was having both articles and poetry published quite regularly. We were a bit over-awed by the people in the Club who'd written books and one in particular who talked about her visits to New York on promotion tours.

"Don't believe everything you hear about America," she told us. "I've never come to any harm over there."

As we got to know more about her we realised all this was true. She would never allow anybody to sit in her chair. A new member doing so unwittingly would soon learn to sit somewhere else.

At that time there was a campaign about adults who couldn't read, the Adult Literacy programme, and Stella and I were asked to volunteer to teach people. One of my students was a man who wanted to be a nurse, but because of his problem with reading he wasn't able to study or take exams. He had a wife and child. I'd go once a week to Prescot where he lived. He had no idea about vowels. I made up stories with words that were spelt the same but not pronounced in the same way. At the progress meetings there was a woman who talked everybody down. The person she had was doing so well.

"It's a wonder they have the chance to get a word in," somebody remarked.

"She lives up to her name," I said to Stella.

"Why? What is her name?"

"Yelland! One of the men told me. Yelland!"

· Chapter Twenty ·

After we'd been in the Writers' Club a couple of years we heard about the Summer School at Swanwick. It was too late for us to book for that year but friends who were there promised to write envelopes for us and leave them in the basket with all the others so that we'd get Application Forms the next year.

"Remember to send the forms back right away," they told us, "otherwise you won't get in."

It's a little easier now but there was fearful competition for places at Swanwick in those days. At our first try we only managed to get onto the waiting list, but eventually we did get places.

It was so exciting meeting people at Derby station with labels on their cases; 'The Writers' Summer School'; drinking tea in the station cafe as we waited for the coaches to take us on to Swanwick and being asked, "What have you had published?" In those days all I could boast of were the letters I had had published in magazines and newspapers. At that time, these didn't really count as being published. It is different nowadays.

Stella and I shared a room that first year and went to every class, every talk, every discussion group, every lecture, every workshop, afraid to miss out on anything. Newcomers always behave like this at Swanwick, but they soon learn to take things a little less seriously.

Tuesday afternoon was set aside for outings: visiting a nearby stately home, walking through Dove Dale or somewhere, or going with the coach party to one of the factories in Derby for seconds or discontinued lines in clothing or pottery. Some people did none of these things but stayed put and had a swim or caught up with sleep. As I got wiser, this is what I did myself on Swanwick Tuesdays, to recharge my batteries.

On top of everything else, each night there was dancing from 10pm till 1am. No wonder we were exhausted by the end of the week. But like everybody else there, once we'd been to Swanwick we were determined to go every year, no matter what.

One of the workshops I went to that first summer was about Picture Scripts, a story to be told as a strip cartoon. When I got home I had a go myself and sent my effort out but it came back.

When a radio station opened in Liverpool people started sending scripts in – stories and poetry and short features. Stella and I tried our luck there too. When she had some of her work accepted and I read out a humorous article on air we felt we'd arrived. Radio Merseyside was a great inspiration for new writers.

From then on, I went to Swanwick every year. Whatever course I'd taken at the School, that was what I concentrated on when I got home: short stories, ghost stories, children's stories. But all were rejected. Still the only things I managed to get published were letters to the editor, and three times a year I had an article in the Trefoil magazine though they didn't pay me for them. These were mostly about Guild outings describing the usual mishaps on these occasions: coaches that were late or got lost or broke down miles from home or (as on one trip) failed to turn up at all! Being Guides, we took it all in our stride.

On the home front, Marion and Peter had bought a caravan which was sited in a caravan park in Wales. It was half-way up a mountain in Penmaenwawr and very secluded. The first night we stayed in the caravan we slept on settees, one each side of the table. In the middle of the night I was wakened by a bang. Leslie had rolled off the seat and was lying on the floor still fast asleep in his sleeping-bag and blankets. Next day we realised that the seats made into a double-bed which was safer!

We were having holidays again at last. Leslie didn't like going to hotels and thought all boarding houses were like the one we'd stayed in during the war.

"They're different now," we all tried to tell him, but it was no use. Once he got an idea in his head nothing and no-one could budge it. Alongside Marion's caravan he built a nest box for the blue-tits. We weren't there to see it but the people in the next caravan said that when the time came twelve chicks had fledged from Leslie's nest box. That pleased him no end.

Over the years we had some lovely times in the different caravans Marion had, which were regularly changed for more luxurious models. One was at a place in Anglesey called Newborough and a shore called Blackrock Sands.

"It's like the Continent there," we were told.

The sky was as blue, the sands as golden, the sea as clear as the Mediterranean. We'd had a few dips when a wave knocked me flat on my face and I began to realise that I was not as young as I thought I was! There was a Nature Reserve nearby with rare plants and exotic butterflies. Leslie was in his element.

"Remember that peacock butterfly in the porch?"

"Yes, I do."

I'd noticed it in the porch one morning, and carefully kept the door closed wanting him to see it too, otherwise he'd say,

"You're kidding me. Peacocks don't come this far north."

It flew away happily – as far as I could tell – when I eventually released it from the porch.

The next caravan Marion got was in Bentham in North Yorkshire. We had some good times there too, but they didn't go on for ever. Visiting Lancaster one day, I met a Trefoil Guild member who had moved away from Liverpool.

"How nice to meet you. Did you retire to here?"

"No, we live in Carnforth."

"We're in a caravan in Bentham."

We talked for a while (with our husbands waiting impatiently).

"I'd better go. See you at the Conference. It's at Carlisle, isn't it."

When they moved, Trefoil members always found a new group to join, and if there wasn't one they'd start one themselves.

"Thought you were going to be nattering to her all day," Leslie grumbled afterwards.

"It'll be different at the weekend when the others come, and you go fishing."

"You'll have Marion to talk to."

"While you and Peter fish to your heart's content.'"

"Let's go and find somewhere to eat. That chap told me of a good place."

"Yes, Mary told me about it too."

· Chapter Twenty-one ·

It was Christmas Day when Eric brought his girl friend Erica to meet the family.

"He's going to marry that girl," I told Leslie.

"You don't know."

"I'll bet you he does."

"You're very sure, considering you don't believe in gambling."

"I am. Has he ever brought a girl home before?"

"No."

"There you are then."

Over the years Leslie had been through all the types of vehicles from a bike to a motorcycle, and then a larger one which, being second-hand, gave him a lot of trouble. If he was late coming home, he'd be walking it. Then it was a bike with a side-car and after that a car, a three-wheeler Reliant. Thinking that this was the best he'd ever have, he didn't change the licence. Eventually he bought a brand new Mini Traveller. It was then that he discovered that with a proper car he would have to take his driving test.

Leslie paid for Eric's driving lessons and once Eric had passed, Leslie had to take the test too. After being on the road all his life! Now it was Eric who had to take his father through it and prepare him for the test. Until

Leslie had safely passed, Eric had the use of the car. If he was out late his Dad would worry about him (and the car).

Eric and Erica used to take me to the Writers' Club. One night we were just five minutes from home on a main road when a car came out of a side road and crashed into us. We finished up in hospital where we were treated for minor wounds but no serious damage had been done and we were allowed to go home. Erica's parents came and took us home. Stella and her husband Hal called to find out what had happened as she had been expecting to join me at the Writers' Club that night.

For me it was like history repeating itself.

"I'm glad I have no more children if this is the way we meet the future in-laws," I said to Stella.

After Leslie had made sure we were all right, he thought of his precious car, and whose fault the accident was.

"It wasn't the driver's fault." A woman who had seen it from the window came running out to testify.

When the police arrived at the scene, the position of the two cars confirmed this.

Erica's father recommended a solicitor and we received compensation. I bought a new sewing machine with some of the money – a *Jones*, of course – the other one was really too heavy for me to lift by then.

A month later I had an attack of sciatica which the doctor said was delayed shock from the accident.

Leslie eventually passed his driving test and obtained a new licence. He and his work-mate used to take turns driving to work. One morning he arrived to pick Leslie up in a terrible state.

"I've knocked a dog over – it ran out in front of me."

"Is it dead?"

"I don't think so – it's eyes are open."

"We'd better go and see." And off they went.

"It is dead. What shall I do about it?"

"You'll have to report it to the police."

He went to the police and explained what had happened.

"It's a big dog with black spots."

"We've heard about that one before. There won't be any comeback."

"Ooh! I'm glad about that."

It seems the dog had regularly been running out into the main road. Men going to work had complained about it. No-one seemed to know who owned the dog.

In 1973 Eric and Erica were married. Evelyn and I made hats of net for the wedding. On the day, when the car came to fetch me I was still in the bath and we had to send it away and go later in the mini. But we made it in time. Indeed, when we arrived the bride from the earlier wedding service was just coming out of the church so we were able to mix in with her crowd inconspicuously.

With both the children married, it was very quiet at home. So at the Trefoil Guild when they asked for a volunteer to join the committee of the Standing Conference of Women's Organisations I said I'd do it.

Most of the churches and clubs were represented.

The Chairman was the ex-headmistress of a posh school and she wore a chain of office like the Lord Mayor. Others were business women, and political figures. I felt like a fish out of water. After many months some of them were beginning to talk to me. At a Christmas party at the Liberal Club the headmistress even condescended to ask my opinion about something. I felt I'd arrived. But at the district party with all the fancy expensive clothes on display, I sat at the table with somebody quite as humble as I was. After the speaker – Edwina Currie, no less – had finished, we sat together and compared notes.

"Did you hear them at the AGM at the Town Hall?"

"The way they were calling all the politicians they didn't agree with?"

"We'll be like the Three Wise Monkeys."

"What's that then?"

"It's a Japanese poem I heard at school . . ."

O'er the door of the sacred temple
They sit in their wisdom, the three.
The little deaf monkey,
The little dumb monkey,
And the monkey who cannot see.
With their eyes shut to evil,
Ears that hear only the right,
Lips that are dumb to scandal,
They sit in their silent might.

· Chapter Twenty-two ·

The years seemed to be flying. So much was happening. Marion had another boy, and Erica also gave birth to a boy. She and Eric had bought a house a long way away from us, and now they decided to come back to Roby.

Stella and I were going to Swanwick every year. We were so compatible, we thought alike, and saw the funny side of things. I felt so smug having left the illness behind me, apart from a few colds which most people have. But on a coach trip to Windermere we were only half way there when I began to feel sick.

"Are you all right?" a friend asked. "You look like a ghost."

It was a relief to get out of the coach and the day was spent in the boat shelter by the lake with friends bringing cups of tea. It was teeming rain all the time.

Another day out with the family Erica had brought buns with hamburgers and I was sick again, blaming the hamburgers which I hadn't eaten before. So it went on with different food until it seemed nothing agreed with me. Visiting the doctor, he thought it could be a stomach ulcer. The medicine he gave me didn't work so I had to pay a visit to the ENT hospital for tests. The doctor had asked me if there was anything else I hadn't told him, anything different. The only thing I could think of was that one night climbing up the steps of a van I'd fallen backwards. In the hospital they asked me did I ever have dizzy spells.

"Only when I wake up in the night with the room going round and round and a throbbing in one ear."

After many tests including pints of water down each ear and months of visiting the hospital, I was given the verdict.

"It's Meniers disease."

"I've never heard of it."

"It upsets the balance in the middle ear," they told me. "That's why you feel dizzy. There's no cure, but it can be kept under control with tablets."

But even with tablets I'd sometimes lose my balance. One night I was being taken to the Writers' Club by Stella and Hal and was going up the steps of his motor caravan when I fell backwards. That was one of the worst falls I'd had. Stella was wonderful. Falling in the house, I'd only have to ring her and she'd be round as soon as she could. Sometimes I'd really injure myself falling and when this happened Stella's daughter who was a nurse would come round too to patch me up.

I missed Evelyn a lot when she died, and Stella helped fill the gap she'd left in my life. I felt we were soul-mates, Stella and I.

Although the Meniers disease slowed me down a bit, it didn't stop me from doing the things I'd always done.

"Slow down," Elsie, my friend from over the road, used to say to me, and some friends still say it today, but it's just the nature of the beast I'm afraid. I can't slow down.

When the Horticultural Society had a display of fruit

and flowers in the school, all the family went. Stella and Hal were there too. Being fond of gardening, Stella and I were persuaded to join the Society. I tried to coax Leslie to join too.

"That chap you know at work was there – he talked about roses."

"He gave me some tips on roses, but he's retired now."

"But you're keen on roses, and he's a champion grower, he wins all the prizes."

"You know very well I'm into clematis now."

So I gave up. We all listened to Percy Thrower on Gardener's Question Time on the radio, so the societies in the district got together and arranged a visit from the panel. We all went along. It was very nice to see the experts in the flesh after only hearing their voices.

Leslie had always been a little deaf. Working in the shipyard with no protection from all the racket hadn't helped. As he got older the deafness got worse. In the shipyard the men were not allowed to stop for tea in the middle of the morning. One day some of the joiners were having an illicit cuppa when the foreman was heard coming down the alleyway. The other men melted away and left Leslie there on his own to face the music.

"You know you're not supposed to stop for tea," he said. "How come you didn't escape with the others?"

"I never heard you. But we're not children. Why shouldn't we have a cup of tea if we want one?"

The foreman went off without another word.

When the others came back, Leslie asked them, "What are you, men or mice, running away like that?"

"He's right," someone said. "They have their tea-break in the office – why can't we have one too?"

So they did. They knew very well they wouldn't be sacked over it, they were such a reliable gang, staying to finish a job when necessary.

At dinner times the men went to the galley for their tea, but on foreign ships where the chef didn't understand English, he wouldn't let them make a brew for themselves. Trying to explain what they wanted was difficult. This particular man conveyed to them that he understood what was needed. He went off and came back with a huge bucket of tea for the men! They didn't ask *him* again!

I tried to persuade my husband to get a hearing aid but he wouldn't. Everywhere we went, I acted as his interpreter. I remember how once in a TV shop he got very annoyed with the manager.

"But you promised it would be ready two days ago . . ." He got very frustrated and began to shout. "You shouldn't make promises that you've no intention of keeping."

The man threatened to call the police.

"He's very deaf," I explained, trying to calm both men down. "That's why he shouts."

"I'll get it done as soon as possible," the shop manager agreed, though this time he did not give us a dead-line. Perhaps the incident had made him think about it.

· Chapter Twenty-three ·

When I first went to the Summer School at Swanwick, the place was very different from the way it is today. Stella and I shared a room in the Garden House. The beds were placed end-to-end making us feel like a pair of book-ends.

Unlike today when we have free tea and coffee making facilities on every landing, the first room on the left in the Garden House was used as a tea-making room for the staff where they'd dish out tea in the morning at 1d a cup. Stella and I took turns in going down from the second floor as soon as the waking alarm sounded to collect our tea. At night after the staff had gone, people would make tea in the kitchen – it was always the women, of course! Sometimes the Ascot in the kitchen would boil over and then the men would be called to help. We'd take cups off the table laid for breakfast but had to wash and replace them before we went to bed, leaving everything as we'd found it.

Table tennis was played in the vinery with bunches of grapes dangling overhead. When it rained, umbrellas and macs were needed to move around between lectures and classes. There were no covered walkways then.

Swanwick was the thing I really looked forward to each year more than anything else. As for many others, it was the highlight of my life. Each year I'd try out something new in the way of classes and courses – short stories, articles, writing for children, radio plays – there was so much to choose from.

As a family, we still went to the caravan at Bentham, playing games on the way to keep the children amused in the car, and once we were there I played cricket and rounders with them. "You throw too hard, Grandma," they'd complain.

Leslie had a job though one in which his skills were not needed and neither were his tools. He hadn't really wanted it. It was promotion and he didn't really like it, he drew the plans for the work but he was persuaded to take it. Some of the other men didn't like it that an older man was given the job. They thought it should have gone to a younger chap. One of them actually said as much to his face, but Leslie said, "If you want the job we will go to the boss together and you can have it." He backed out at that.

Another of them said, "These old fellows should retire," mentioning by name a man who'd had a slight stroke which made him a bit slower.

"Look here," my husband said, "that man was a brilliant joiner, he knows more about the job than you ever will."

"I didn't know that."

"And by the way, I'm one of these old fellows."

"I can't believe it. I hope I look as good as you when I'm old."

"You might never make it, with your life style."

This man went out every night drinking and every dinner time too.

Leslie was sixty-seven when he retired. Knowing we'd only have the Old Age Pension coming in, he'd wanted to stay on as long as he could. Like so many men, he always hated shopping, going straight for what we needed without looking at any alternatives. When he retired he changed from a reluctant shopper to an enthusiastic one, searching the supermarket shelves for bargains or 'money off' coupons. I still got my chocolates every Friday but now I chose my own.

For some time we had been going to Wales every Saturday looking for a cottage to buy, but the places were mostly terrible and the Estate Agents' descriptions were not anything like the places we were sent to view. There was one in Anglesey that we never found although we looked for it a number of times.

Eventually I said, "We might as well give up. You don't want to be renovating the place, not at your age."

So we just satisfied ourselves with talking about the places we'd looked at.

"Remember that one where the agent said, 'You don't need a key'?"

"He was right – it was a ruin. We stepped in over the one wall that was left standing."

"You won't be needing that book you bought about raising goats."

"Not now, no – it was just a dream."

A dream that didn't come true.

So we left it at that and decided to stay put. But going on trips with the Trefoil Guild made me think that we should have looked nearer home, in Lancashire perhaps. We did try a couple of places. One was very intriguing –

a great setting for a mystery novel. The place had been empty for weeks but it was fully furnished and looked as though someone was still living there. As if the family had just gone out for a walk, perhaps, and never come back, leaving everything exactly as it was. We couldn't find out what had happened. Where had they gone? Why had they left all their possessions behind? It was quite spooky.

The agent couldn't tell us anything about it, or at least that was his story. He knew nothing about it, he said.

"We can't afford it anyway."

"It's too lonely there for me, too isolated."

So this time we really did give up and decided to stay here for the rest of our lives.

When the caravan was sold, Leslie was quite happy not to be going on holiday any longer, though he didn't mind me going off on the annual Trefoil outings, and the week at Swanwick. It seemed as if a quiet routine was all he needed in life with the daily 'excitement' of a trip to the shops enough for him. But it didn't do for me.

The week at Swanwick with Stella each August was great. Although she is a good deal younger than I am, it doesn't seem to matter. And now that Leslie was retired, it was much easier to prepare for Summer School than it had been when he was working. In those days, I had to work out all his meals for the week and leave intructions for him. He'd have a day with Marion while I was away and I'd make sure she and Eric would call in on their Dad now and again during my absence.

The pattern of our lives had stayed the same for a very long time. Now everything was changing.

People were dying, others moving away. Anfield Guild had lost so many members that it had to close down. The few that were left belonged to the Mothers Union and I was invited to their annual outings. On one of them it was thrilling to meet a woman who had gone to our school. She had been a wonderful swimmer winning all the trophies. She had been a few classes above me at school and I'd only known her by sight, admiring her, the way you do, as a brilliant swimmer and a senior. To meet her and talk to her more than fifty years later was a great joy to me. We chatted about the swimming galas we'd been to. Strangely enough, when she left school she'd worked in Ogden's, the other big tobacco factory in Liverpool, though not as a stripper.

· Chapter Twenty-four ·

Fate or whatever it is that shapes our lives decided that I was being too complacent and should be shaken up a bit. The trouble started as a pain which gradually increased as the day wore on till by bedtime it was so bad I couldn't sleep and had to get up and walk about.

"What can I do?" Leslie kept asking. "Is there nothing I can do to help?"

"Nothing," I groaned. "I'll be in hospital in the morning, that's for sure."

The doctor came and examined me. "I'm afraid you have shingles." (Why do doctors use that expression, '*I'm afraid*' when it's the patients who should be afraid!)

"I thought that was some kind of roofing material, shingles."

"Shingles is also a very painful illness," he told me, writing out prescriptions for some soothing lotion and painkillers though their effectiveness only lasted about two hours after which I was up and out of bed again pacing round the room.

They had warned me that shingles lasts a long time, indeed that in some cases the pain goes on for life. It began to seem as if this was happening with me.

"Why don't you go to that doctor I went to with my frozen shoulder?" Marion said. "That acupuncturist."

And so I did. He had his surgery in a private house. In

contrast with the local GP's surgery, for a consultation with the acupuncturist the patient would sit opposite him in a comfortable chair. He'd been to China to study acupuncture. When I enquired, he told me how much it would cost for each session with him and that it might take eight sessions but if after three there was no sign of improvement then it meant the treatment wasn't going to work.

"It doesn't matter how much it costs," Leslie said, "you can't go on like this."

We had some laughs going for acupuncture. There were people waiting to see him who were trying to give up smoking. They would be sitting in the waiting room with a fan of needles sticking out of both ears, looking like spacemen.

The acupuncture worked for me, and thankfully the shingles pain has not come back.

1987 was our Golden Wedding anniversary.

"Are you doing anything about it?" various friends were asking.

"Oh the children will probably take us out for a meal,"I told them.

On the day, a golden rosebush was delivered from a nursery, and flowers from the florist.

Marion rang and said Eric would pick us up at six o'clock.

"Where is it we're going, Marion? Have you booked a table?"

"Wait and see."

Later in the day, a pal brought a box of Cadbury's

Gold chocolates.

Eric and Erica came to collect us. The grandchildren were very excited and eager to tell us something but were shushed up. It was very mysterious.

When we arrived at Marion's, the house was full of people: my closest friend Stella, Elsie, Margery from school, Alice from the Trefoil Guild, and other friends, neighbours and relations.

I stood there clutching my box of chocolates thinking to open them after the meal in the restaurant that I thought we'd be going to.

But the party was *here* – Marion and Erica had arranged it all. What a wonderful surprise!

"It was so difficult trying to keep it secret . . ."

"The children were dying to tell you . . ."

"I noticed in the car, but never expected this."

The men had ferried those guests without transport of their own. It was a huge combined effort, and all in secret.

"We were a bit scared in case it was too much for you," Marion told me afterwards. "But you were going round your guests kissing them and shaking hands like the blooming Queen Mother!"

The Hillsborough disaster affected everyone in Liverpool whether or not they were interested in football.

It was Saturday April 15th 1989. Leslie and I had settled down to our usual quiet afternoon. Marion and Erica were both working. Eric had taken his son Jonathan and Marion's boy Jeffrey and a friend of his to Sheffield to watch a football game.

Leslie was listening to the Radio through head-phones and watching the snooker on TV with the sound turned off. He interrupted my reading by shouting, "There's trouble at Hillsborough."

"What's happened?"

"The crowd at the Liverpool end have invaded the pitch and the game has been stopped."

"Stopped? It must have only just started."

Leslie turned the TV to another station, and the news grew very worrying with garbled accounts from different people about what had happened. But everyone's version told the same terrible story: Liverpool supporters were being crushed to death. And the number of casualties kept rising. It was terrifying, particularly as all the males in the family were right there in the middle of the unfolding tragedy.

The Liverpool fans were at the wrong end of the ground, it had been said when the game had been planned, but no notice had been taken of the complaints.

"What if they are among the dead, our lads, and we are still here?" Leslie said. "All those young people."

"Yes, the toll is going up all the time."

We decided to go and see Marion. On the bus, she'd heard about the trouble, but no details.

Most of the reporters were blaming the Liverpool fans and one from The Sun newspaper even said that the fans were looting the pockets of the dead. We heard afterwards that what they were actually doing was going through their pockets to try to find some means of identify them.

It was hours – it seemed like a lifetime – before Eric

was able to get to a phone and ring his wife to say they were all safe, and that they'd be home as soon as possible. It was such a relief for us all, but not everyone was so lucky. For many families, a phone call from Sheffield that evening brought nothing but sorrow and despair.

We didn't hear all that had happened to Eric and the boys until next day, after Eric had felt a compulsion to go to Anfield.

"It seemed as though the whole of Liverpool had turned up to mourn," he said.

Not being able to get near himself, he passed over Jonathan's scarf to be tied on one of the gates along with hundreds of other tokens of grief. "The field was full of flowers," he said.

Then he told us what had happened at the match . . .

We'd started out early, the four of us, to be there in good time. We'd taken sandwiches and drinks.

"I stopped at a garage to fill up with petrol," Eric told us.

"You're lucky," a bloke at the next pump said. "It's a nice day for the Semi-final."

"Any day's a nice day if we win!"

We had some fun with Everton fans on their way to their match. As we Approached the M62 there was a huge traffic jam. Near Sheffield, as we came off the motorway, Police were stopping coaches, pulling them to one side and taking away any alcoholic drinks from fans.

I arrived at the road I'd used last year, parked the car and joined the happy crowd. We'd agreed that if we got split up during the game we'd meet at a certain garage afterwards.

We arrived at the ground and found the four turnstiles at the Leppings Road were congested because there was no control of the queues packed round them.

As more and more people arrived the crowd were squashed tighter and tighter. Jonathan and I were together but the other two boys were some 10ft away.

As the time for the kick-off approached, the ones behind began to push again, frantic to get inside the ground before the game started, and not realising that the congestion problem was becoming dangerous.

At this point I pulled Jonathan away, we stood against a fence at the side and this probably saved us.

"We'll wait here for the others – I've got their tickets so they'll be bound to look for us."

There's a set of iron gates about 2ft away from the turn-stiles. Some of the supporters took it upon themselves to close these gates to relieve the congestion by preventing any more getting through. This seemed to be working until the police inside the grounds decided to open the main gate. Of course, the crowd surged towards it and poured into the ground, hundreds of them.

Because I had their tickets, Jonathan and I stayed where we were to wait for the boys. After a while police closed the gate, thus creating more congestion among those left outside.

Then the police opened the gates again and the crowd pushed in until nearly everyone was inside. The boys must have been pushed through by the crowd *without tickets*!

We went in, visited the toilets, bought a programme and started down the tunnel into the ground. I remembered from last year that this would bring us out on the centre terrace area which always gets very crowded. So, fortunately for us, we turned back and went to the side entrance.

When we arrived at the side entrance we found that the match had already started. But instead of watching the game, my attention was drawn to the centre terrace which was divided from the the side by a high fence. To try to escape from the crush, people were climbing this fence – just a mass of people. The thing was: the look on their faces was sheer terror! They were struggling to save themselves, fighting for their lives.

When the officials realised what was happening, the game was stopped. I noticed the police carrying out a young boy of maybe ten years old. Next thing, they'd started giving him the Kiss of Life.

At this point I realised this was no ordinary football incident. This was something serious. More people were on the pitch now. Fans were desperately tearing down the bill-boards lining the pitch. Nottingham fans, not understanding what was going on, started boo-ing. They thought the trouble was simply a fight. They soon fell silent as they watched the Liverpool fans using the bill-boards as stretchers to carry the dead and injured out of the crush. Then, knowing that they themselves were quite helpless and unable to do anything, they started applauding.

Worried sick for their safety, Jonathan and I went back to the turnstiles to look for our two boys. What greeted us was the frightening sight of bodies lying everywhere. Some were being given the Kiss of Life. Others were crying and screaming with friends trying comfort and help them. Although there was no blood to be seen, it was quite obvious that among the injured were many dead.

"Where's Jeff!" Jonathan shouted.

The shirts of the dead had been pulled over their faces. We moved among the bodies thinking we would be able to identify Jeff by his trainers.

By this time I began to panic. Where was Jeff? What if we couldn't find him and his mate? How could I go home to my sister without her son? And his pal's parents too – what was I to say to all of them?

I thought if we went up into the stand above the gruesome scene we might be able to spot the two boys. We climbed the stairs but as we reached the first floor corridor behind the stand I was horrified to see dead bodies everywhere.

In desperation, we decided to go to the meeting place as arranged. Jonathan was very distressed as there were more dead and injured outside too.

At the garage, the pre-arranged spot, we began to wait hopefully. That was the longest 45 minutes of my life. At last two familiar figures appeared running towards us.

"Thank God you're here!"

"Thank God you're all right, both of you!"

It turned out afterwards that if we hadn't had to go and wait for them we'd have been in the thick of it.

We were walking down the road towards the car thankful to be safe, all of us, when a man stopped us and said, "Do you want to come to my house and ring your family?"

The house was already full of people waiting to use his phone. He and his wife were giving everyone cups of tea while they waited. They refused to take any money for either the tea or the phone calls. Later we heard that other Sheffield people were doing the same, doing what they could to help.

The boys were traumatised by what had happened. They didn't want to talk about it, but eventually they told us that they'd been passed over heads and pulled over the fence, by Nottingham fans.

That is Eric's first-hand account of that terrible event.

On the way home in the car he was listening to the Radio and saying, "That's not right. No, that's not what happened. They've got it all wrong."

There's a big memorial at Anfield today, and fans have tried without success to get one put up at Hillsborough too.

It has been said that the fans were drunk but most of the pubs were closed. Drink had been taken from everyone beforehand by the police. The fans of both sides did more for the injured than the police, getting them out of the crush and into ambulances as quickly as possible.

When Stella's husband retired from work, it was understandable that they'd be spending more time together, so we didn't see as much of each other as before. We'd already left the Writers Club and now Stella stopped going to Swanwick.

For a couple of years, I didn't go either. When various Swanwick friends wrote to ask why I wasn't going any more I told them I'd miss Stella too much.

One of them wrote: "Come by yourself, Flo. You know plenty of people there. You're scarcely going to be lonely."

The family were encouraging me to start going to Swanwick again too. Even my husband joined the chorus: "You might as well go – you know how much you used to enjoy it." I think he was looking for a peaceful week without me!

And so I booked a place at Swanwick again.

It was strange without Stella, strange going into the dance at night on my own. The only seat I could find was on the edge of the platform. As the music started up, Joy Peach came dancing by and stopped beside me and said, "Come on, come and dance!" I'd seen Joy before but had never spoken to her. That small gesture of hers made all the difference to me. I felt part of the scene again instead of conspicuously alone. Joy has a lot of friends at Swanwick and now I was part of her circle too.

After a couple of years talking about things I remembered, I was being urged to write my memories. But at the Writers Club and at Swanwick too we had always been told that it's only the memoirs of the famous that get published. That no-one is interested the life story of the Little Woman in the Street.

Inspite of this, when I read an advertisement in the Liverpool Echo which said: "Do you want to write your autobiography?" I rang the telephone number given and enrolled for the seminar at the Central Library. The course was very good and I was amazed to hear about all the Writing Clubs and Workshops around the city. I joined one called Rosco.

Compared with the more modest projects I'd been used to tackling – poetry, letters-to-editors and articles – the prospect of writing my life story was a formidable one. A whole book! Me! With my one-finger-only typing technique! I'd never do it.

I tried to find somebody to help. If I'd confided in them, Eric or Marion might have known someone, a student perhaps or an unemployed teacher. But so far I hadn't told anyone of my plan apart from the Rosco group, and of the parts I'd read to them they were very encouraging.

By now, at Swanwick Joy and I were close friends. Each morning we'd sit together at the eight o'clock Lift Up Your Hearts service and then have a walk round the lake together before breakfast. With so many people there, we might not catch sight of one another again all day, though we always met up at the late night dancing.

As we walked round the lake, I'd tell Joy various things about my childhood, my family, my life at the tobacco factory, and sometimes start quoting poems I'd learnt at school or burst out singing songs we'd sung in the church choir or at concerts in those distant days.

"Listen!" Joy said, "Don't keep *telling* me all this – you must write it down. It's a lost world you're describing, Flo. It's fascinating. It deserves to be published."

Joy has an Amstrad word processor. "If you send me a chunk as it's ready, a few pages, a chapter, I'll type it up for you and send it back straight away for you to correct or whatever. And then you can send me the next chapter."

"D'ye mean it?"

"Course I do."

"Well, if you don't think it's any good you must say so. You must tell me. OK?"

And so I got going. With Joy behind me saying fiercely, "Right, Flo – now I want a chapter a week."

That gave me the incentive to get down to work. And it was so encouraging seeing the properly typed sheets arriving week-by-week from Whitby.

"You're wasting your time," Leslie said. "I've read in the Echo that half of Liverpool are writing their memoirs. It'll never get published."

"You never know," I told him.

"Well, what's the harm if it keeps you happy."

So that was it. I kept on writing.

· Chapter Twenty-five ·

It seems strange that we only met members of Prescot Trefoil Guild in different towns at conferences, because Prescot is not very far from Huyton. Meeting Alice, the Chairman, a few times, she invited our Guild to join theirs at the annual outing. Some of us did, and I spent most of the day with Alice. Alighting from the coach on our return, I was just in time to see my bus driving away.

"It'll be ages before the next one. What will you do?"

"There's a phone box, look – I'll ring my husband."

"You can ring from our house," Alice said.

And so I did.

"That's a lovely picture," I said, as I waited for Leslie to collect me.

"It's tapestry," said Alice, taking it down from the wall. "I've been doing it for a few years now, tapestry. These ones are ready to be framed."

"I love scenes of country cottages."

When he arrived, Leslie was introduced to Alice and her husband, Jim.

That was the start of a great friendship. We used to meet for lunch in one another's houses, Alice and I. The first time she visited me, when she was ready to leave Leslie offered to drive her home without me having to ask him. With other friends, he usually waited a few visits before offering them a lift home, but not with Alice.

Alice decided to learn to crochet and became an expert and made beautiful things. All this was before I'd joined the Writing Group at the library which would come to take up a good deal of my time. Gradually we stopped meeting, but we are still best friends today, Alice and I.

Leslie began to have trouble walking. He said his legs weren't painful, "but they just wont walk." He didn't go out or drive the car any longer, so I had to take over the jobs he'd always done like going to the newsagents twice a day for a paper, and it meant doing the shopping alone.

One morning he was panic stricken. "I can't get out of bed, Flo – it's my back."

I rang the doctor who gave him pills and arranged for a specialist to come. He advised Eric to put a board under his dad's mattress which helped a bit. Leslie was in bed for a week. He'd never liked having meals in bed but he put up with it. The specialist told him he'd be taken to Whiston Hospital one day a week for five weeks for tests. Leslie wasn't keen.

"It's all women," he grumbled after his first visit. "No other men.'"

One day he came home with a piece of birthday cake.

"There was a birthday party and they were all kissing me."

"Not many men your age are so lucky!"

On the last day of his treatment he said he didn't want to wait for the ambulance. "Get a taxi and come for me."

The tests were all negative except for a hiatus hernia that only needed a careful diet. Leslie didn't believe the results. He thought there was something serious that they weren't telling him. As he'd had such good health all his life, I suppose it was extra hard for him to cope with the pain and the difficulties. His only experience of hospital was at the age of 80 when he went in for the operation on his (ordinary) hernia, from which he soon recovered.

I kept going to the meetings at the library and was always home at a certain time, near enough, until one day I was late. Leslie was waiting at the gate for me.

"Where've you been?"

"I just missed the bus."

"I thought something had happened to you."

The next week he said, "Here's the money – get a cab home."

I used to like going on the bus, talking to people, but after a while I found it was just as interesting learning about the cab drivers and their families. They used to ask what I was going to the library for.

"I'm writing a book."

They were all very interested and usually came out with the same comment: "I could write a book."

"I'm sure you could, with all the different folk you've had in your cab."

"Will you ever finish yours?"

"I hope so."

While I was struggling to keep going on the book, writing each page two or three times and then discarding most of them before sending the chapter to Joy to type up, Leslie would be saying, "You're wasting your time, it's never going to be published."

"Don't keep saying that." I felt he should have been encouraging me.

"It's only because I don't want to see you disappointed, love, after all this work."

We went on in this way for some time, quietly bickering over my writing.

"I've got a headache," he said one day.

"That's not like you – you never have a headache."

"Well, I've got one now."

The headache got worse.

"He wont have the doctor," I told Marion when she called next day.

"Oh yes he will," she said, and she rang for him.

The doctor said it was migraine and that he'd call again in a few days. "Let me know if it gets any worse," he told me.

It did get worse. The very next day it got worse. When the doctor came Leslie was in agony.

"I'll ring the hospital."

"I'm not going to hospital. Can't *you* give me something?"

"Afraid not."

Leslie's eye was closing. In the ambulance he said, "This road's terrible – I can feel every bump."

The men were very good to him. They lifted him out of the chair and got him lying down comfortably.

"You wont feel it as much that way," they said.

In the hospital ward a man was sitting on a chair. He'd had to vacate his bed for the new patient.

I'd rung Marion before we left home and she arrived at the hospital soon after us. I was glad she was there because we had a long wait before the doctors could say what was the matter with Leslie. We felt quite helpless. He was in so much pain. It was a few hours before someone even came to take down his details.

"Never mind all that," Leslie kept saying. "Give me something for the pain, for God's sake."

"You have to see the specialist," they told him.

Marion had rung Eric and now he arrived at the hospital. And the specialist came, saying Leslie had had a slight stroke.

"Well, I've had a good innings," Leslie said when he was told.

For the next fortnight Marion and Eric took it in turns to take me to the hospital every night. Then Leslie was allowed home. Gradually his eye was opening again and he found he could still see with it. The specialist had said this might happen but it was unusual. The hospital were very pleased about it.

And we were all delighted!

· Chapter Twenty-six ·

So we settled down with a Home Help coming (or not coming!) every morning. We could never rely on them. Leslie wouldn't let me help him.

"What if you collapsed?" he'd say. "I couldn't do anything."

When they failed to turn up, I'd ring the Home Help office, but it didn't make much difference.

"Who d'you think we'll have today?"

"Maybe Number Twenty."

I kept all their names in my diary.

"It's because there are two of you," one of them said. "That's what makes it difficult."

During this time I'd had an eye test and was amazed when the optician said, "I can't give you stronger glasses because you've got cataracts on both eyes."

"I don't believe it. I've got wonderful sight. Always have had."

"I'll send a note to your doctor. He'll make you an appointment at the hospital."

The cataracts were confirmed at the hospital. I was to have one eye done at a time. They'd send for me, they said, and then I'd go in one day and have the operation and the next day I'd be able to take the shade off. But each time I fainted afterwards. I was already taking pills for heart failure.

"See your own doctor when you get home," they told me.

Marion rang the Practice and a lady doctor came. After examining me she said, "It's the hospital you need." And added, "Now!"

"I can't go into hospital. I have to look after my husband."

"I'll be all right," he said.

"It may be for only a few days."

The doctor rang the Social Services and they arranged for Leslie to go into a Respite Home while I was in hospital. It was only two roads away. I packed his things and Marion took him there and then took me on to the hospital. By the time she got home she'd been six hours sorting us out, bless her. A terrible long day for her.

Leslie didn't like the Home at all, but then he didn't like anywhere except his own home. He was only happy in his own house. For one thing, he couldn't bear the noise of all the people talking.

And as for the TV: "It's got no sub-titles," he grumbled. He stayed in his room, worrying about the budgie so in the end they took him home to get it.

During the time that he was recovering from the stroke, I'd kept on writing the first book. I gave the final chapter to Joy at Swanwick that year and she soon sent it back typed and ready to be corrected. And there it was, ready for the publisher. But which publisher? That was the question, how to set about finding a publisher?

As all fellow writers know, it isn't easy, finding a publisher. At my age, I couldn't afford to send the typescript out to one publisher after another, each of whom would probably keep it six months or so before rejecting it. I simply hadn't got time for that.

Then I was told about Susan Westaby who'd published her own books very successfully. I rang her. She came round and took the typescript away to read it. When she brought it back she said, "This should be published. It definitely should." So she decided to take a chance on it, and her gamble has paid off. Susan even thought of the title for me: LIVERPOOL STRIPPER.

"That's misleading," Leslie said, "you're not that sort of woman."

"Maybe not," I said, "but it's what I did all those years." Stripping the tobacco leaves off the stalks. In the cigarette factory.

Eric was with us when the suggestion came up. "It's a good title, Mum. Catchy. Go on, use it."

Susan finished publication of *A Liverpool Stripper* in time for it to come out on Mothering Sunday, which probably helped a lot. I was amazed at the way it sold. Beforehand, I'd thought, Well at least the family will read it.

The day the doctor visited me, she looked at a sore on Leslie's nose and said, "How long have you had that?"

"It's all right," he said. "It heals up for a while and then starts up again."

"We've been telling him to see his doctor about it but he won't."

"Get it seen to," she said on her way out.

An appointment was made in another hospital. They said he needed an operation to remove the sore. He didn't have to wait long. The problem was deep-rooted.

It had to be cut out and skin grafted over it. In a few months it healed very well and visitors used to say,

"It hasn't spoiled your beauty, George."

Apart from close friends, outside the family Leslie was called by his first name, George.

It was a Saturday morning when the next blow came.

Gary, the Home Help, had come to help to get Leslie dressed. He came downstairs. "He can't get out of bed this morning. I'll give him a wash if you'll ring the doctor."

All I got was a message on the Surgery answering machine: "If it's urgent, ring the police. If not, the surgery will be open at 9am on Monday." That wasn't much help!

Gary rang for an ambulance. We arrived at the Royal at ten o'clock and he was transferred to Broadgreen at twelve-thirty. He was there for three weeks and had all the tests it was possible to have. All the results were negative, but Leslie wouldn't believe it.

"There's something they're not telling me, Flo."

"No, they have to tell the patients nowadays, they have to tell them what's wrong," Marion said. "This isn't the nineteen-thirties, Dad, they have to tell you."

But he wouldn't have it. He found it hard to cope with any change, any progress. He was still thinking in terms of pounds, shillings and pence!

We'd been on the waiting list for a stairlift, and it was installed the day before he came out of hospital. It was such a help, and such a relief to me – I no longer had to phone one of the children to help him whenever he needed to go upstairs.

I wasn't so well either. The Meniers Disease had started again, not as bad as before but it upset my sense of balance and I found myself falling over. My legs were quite battle-scarred – more than once I'd had to go and have my wounds stitched up in the hospital.

What with my troubles and his own, Leslie became quite frail and depressed.

"I've had a good innings," he'd say. "I'm ready to go."

"You've got to hang on until September," I'd tell him, "for our Diamond Wedding." I knew the children were planning something big.

Leslie couldn't come to terms with illness. He no longer did anything. The heart had gone out of him.

The crunch came when he said he was feeling very bad but wouldn't stay in bed. The doctor came and suggested he should go into hospital for a few days.

The casualty department of the Royal Hospital was crowded. It's newly built with rows of cubicles on either side, but it was so busy there were people outside in the corridor as well. What with the crowds and the nurses and doctors scurrying around, it reminded me of a busy market. After about an hour it was Leslie's turn to be seen to. Two men came to take blood samples. He didn't like it one bit, and told them so in no uncertain terms. Eventually he was taken into a temporary ward and we were both given food and drink.

It was six o'clock before I managed to get to a phone and ring Marion to come and see her Dad and take me home. Next morning, ringing in to enquire how he was, they said he'd been moved to another ward and that he was much better, so that was a relief.

With all this going on, I'd had to start taking a stronger heart tablet. One particular night I wasn't feeling very well so Eric persuaded me to stay at home while he and Erica went to the hospital. Later, he popped in to tell me that all was well with Leslie and that he hadn't minded me not going to visit him, just for once.

"Is he eating?" I asked.

"Yes, he is."

No matter what had happened to him, Leslie had always had a very good appetite. If he was eating I felt everything must be fine with him. So it was a surprise to be wakened in the early hours with a summons to go to the hospital right away. I rang Eric. He picked me up and collected Marion on the way. Leslie was unconscious and breathing heavily.

"You said he was all right," I said to the nurses.

"We are just as surprised as you are."

We sat there watching him till we were asked to leave the room. Then the doctor came out and said, "I'm sorry we couldn't save him."

Poor Leslie was dead.

I don't remember how we got home, just finding myself at Eric's and going to bed there.

From then on I was like a zombie, unable to walk without help. We blamed the tablets, the shock, the grief, but probably it was just me. All I kept saying was, "I should have gone with you that last night, I should have gone to see him."

Eric and Marion and Erica were very good to me and saw to everything, the funeral and all. Afterwards, when it was all over, I went back home.

Marion had to go away on a course for a week. Eric called in every morning on his way to work. They were all wonderful.

Eric had arranged with Social Services for me to go to the Respite Home for a week to help me recover. So that's what I did.

· Chapter Twenty-seven ·

Two days before I was due to go into the Home, I had another fall and that meant another visit to the hospital for stitches. I arrived at the Home with a bag full of bandages the nurse had given me.

My first impression of Moss View Home was of space and light. Erica came with me. A Sister met us as soon as we entered and took us down a long carpeted corridor to a large room with a wide window looking out to a garden with a rockery and a lawn with paths on all sides and seats to sit on to enjoy the sunshine. The predominant colour was a warm welcoming pink. The walls were pink, the bedding was pink. Each room had a television set, a wardrobe and chest of drawers, one drawer with a lock and key. For each room there was a bathroom with a pink towel and flannel which I found were changed every day. It was wonderfully comfortable.

In the dining room the meals were very good with a choice of menu and small tables, more like a hotel than a nursing home.

Visitors were allowed to come any time. Eric came one night after he'd been to the football match. The staff were so good and patient especially with the usual awkward people like the man in the dining room who complained in a loud voice about everything that was put before him, and the woman who kept demanding a tissue.

"They're very busy," I said.

"You can't get anything in this place, I want it now!"

The first day I was there, the Sister said, "Would you like to come down to the lounge? If you would, I'll come and fetch you."

She took me to a small alcove with three seats on either side where there were five women, four of them asleep in their chairs.

"This is the worst place I've ever been in," said the only one awake.

"Why? Have you been in others?"

"They've had me everywhere."

"Who have?"

"My family."

"Are there many of them, then?"

"Oh yes, and grandchildren too."

This was too depressing and as soon as the tea was brought round, I asked to be taken back to my room and stayed there reading and watching TV.

Before the Home was built, a row of very old Victorian houses had been knocked down and everyone was speculating about what the new building would be. Rumour had it, it was to be a nursing home.

"Not another one, surely."

"There's three in Huyton already."

"They're springing up everywhere."

"Well, there's a lot of old people round here."

One day a new Sister took me to the dining room.

"I'm sorry to hear about your husband – he was a very nice man."

"Thank you."

"Have you still got the budgie?"

"Yes, I'm a bit worried about it. He sulks when either of us is away."

"Tell your son to bring him here, then."

And he did. But Smokey was very sad and silent in the Home.

One morning at breakfast I shared a table with a lady named Irene. During the conversation I told her how friends of mine had been wondering about who owned the Home.

Irene said, "I know the owner."

"So it doesn't belong to Huyton Council – they sent me here. Is it Liverpool, then? Being one road from Huyton, does it come under Liverpool Health Authority?"

"No," she said. "Come down to the lounge and I'll tell you all about it."

Going down to the lounge again to meet Irene, I realised I'd been very mistaken about it before, on that first afternoon. It was very large and separated into three parts (with TV sets in two of them), where patients could sit with others or in couples or by themselves if they wanted to be quiet. Windows ran the whole length of the building. Sitting in the lounge or by the entrance door (as some did) one was able to to see the cars and buses passing on the main road which gave us a good feeling that we belonged to the community still, and were not cut off from life and isolated as some Homes make their patients feel.

When I found Irene in the lounge, she told me she had an hour to talk before she was due at Physiotherapy.

"Does it belong to Huyton Council or Liverpool?" I

asked her again.

"No," she told me. "It's privately owned and very expensive."

"I only had to pay a nominal sum."

"It's owned by a gentleman called Alan Varley who bought up a number of large Victorian houses and converted them into Nursing Homes. They're all good, but being so new, this is the best."

Alan Varley's ambition was to make people who were approaching the end of their lives as happy and comfortable as possible, Irene told me. She said that he is a charming man and visits the Home most days to make sure everything is going well and that the patients are really happy and really comfortable.

"Do you know him?" I asked her.

"Yes, his brother was a friend of my husband."

"Is your husband still alive?"

"No, but we had a wonderful life together, going everywhere." And she went on to tell me that they'd had a furniture business, which took them abroad a lot.

We were interrupted by two men who had come to collect Irene for her Physiotherapy session.

"See you tomorrow," she called as they wheeled her away.

I don't sleep very much nowadays so, as I do at home, rather than lie awake, I put the light on and read. In the early hours, the door opened. I thought they would tell me off for not trying to sleep, but no – "Would you like a cup of tea?" they asked.

The Home owns a mini-bus which can hold eight patients and two helpers. It's used for outings and to take people for eye tests and hospital visits.

On the Wednesday after I arrived there was a choice for us: a trip to Southport or a ceramic class. I decided on the trip and was rather dismayed to find myself seated in the bus next to the lady who had complained so much on my first day. But it was all right – she seemed to have forgotten all her grumbles. On the way she told me she'd been in quite a few Homes and when she was fed up with one her daughters moved her to another.

"You've been here before, then?"

"Yes, twice."

"The others must have been like palaces if they're better than this one."

In Southport we sat in a small cafe by the Marina watching the swans sailing calmly by outside the window. Back in the bus, the driver took us along the Promenade to collect theatre tickets for those who had ordered them, returning before the rush hour.

Next day I met up with Irene again and she told me more about the place. There are two more lounges, and a small room furnished and decorated like an ordinary living room. It's called the Quiet Room where you can sit quietly and feel as though you are in your own home.

"I think the hand-rails in the corridors are a wonderful idea – I've only small spaces to negotiate without them."

"You're lucky to be on your feet, Flo."

"I realise that. Since I've been here I've realised just how lucky I am."

I left the Home with many good wishes and the members of staff saying, "Come back again, next time you need a rest."

· Finally ·

Back home the most urgent job to be done was to take the budgie to the vet and so the first time Marion had a free day from work that's what we did. It turned out the poor thing was suffering from stress (as we all were by then!) but a couple of drops of medicine in his drinking water every night soon did the trick and within a week he was his old self, talking again and chirping away.

After Leslie's death there had been so much to be done, but I hadn't had the strength to begin to tackle any of it. Eric and Marion had spent most of one day sorting out the boxroom which was a formidable task as their father had never thrown anything away.

"What on earth did he want *this* for?" they'd ask as another useless article came to light.

"He always thought it might come in handy. One day."

Over the years, as the boxroom filled up and there was no more room in the cockloft, Leslie would just build another shed.

"The neighbours must think I'm moving," I told them, seeing all that stuff waiting for a skip to be delivered for it to be removed.

To start with, while I adjusted to being on my own, Eric used to call in every morning on his way to work, but after a week or so I told him I'd be all right now.

Jean, our Trefoil chairman, had visited me at the Home bringing flowers and another day Eunice, the secretary, had brought me a book sent by a lady in Canada who'd seen my photograph in the Trefoil magazine and taken the trouble to find out from headquarters how to get in touch with me. She had written her autobiography as well. Like me, she was over eighty when she wrote it. It is a very interesting book.

It was very hard getting used to the idea that my husband would never come home again. Sleeping in the bed we'd shared for so many years, I found myself talking in the early hours of the morning and of course receiving no reply. Moving into the back room has helped a lot. Downstairs it's little things I miss most, the things he always used to do, like testing the batteries for the clocks and radio, opening awkward tins and bottles, things I'd taken for granted for so long.

But I mustn't forget that the children miss him too.

In my lifetime, so many things have changed. A lot of the snobbery and class division have gone and people are judged today not by what they possess but by who they are, what they do with their lives.

And then the technology – who would have dreamt that the day would come when so many amazing gadgets respond to the touch of a button.

It's a shame about the moon which used to be so romantic and magic. Mothers would threaten children who mis-behaved with "You'll be sent to the moon." Since mankind has walked on the moon, its magic is lost.

To my way of thinking, the most amazing changes have taken place in hospitals.

"Can we sit on the bed?" one of my visitors asked nervously.

"Yes, it's very free and easy now. Indeed, two of us stayed up till two in the morning to watch a film on TV."

"It used to be so different, so strict, with no more than two visitors per patient," she said, seeing a nearby bed surrounded by visitors, adults and children and a baby in a pram. "Things certainly have changed."

Patients are treated as people now, as individuals. They can talk to a consultant, for instance, on equal terms without having a Sister as intermediary.

One thing that isn't so good is clothes sizing. Manufacturers now skip a category in women's sizes assuming that within each category – 12, 14, 16 – all of us are the same shape and size. And finding a half-size in shoes is almost impossible.

Now in the spring of 1998 and near the end of my life, I have so much to be thankful for: the wonderful doctor who has kept me going all these years, the friends in the Trefoil Guild who have shown me so much kindness and caring, writers at the Summer School and those at the Liverpool group who keep in touch, and the neighbours I've known for a very long time.

I must also mention my friend Joy Peach as without her generosity and hard work this book would not have been written, and Susan Westaby who is again taking a chance in publishing it.

A BIG THANKYOU TO EVERYONE.